Football For Coaches

Jason Pyott

Football Emotional Intelligence

Football EQ For Coaches

Author: Jason Pyott

Copyright © Jason Pyott (2021)

The right of Jason Pyott to be identified as author of this work has been asserted by the author in accordance with section 77 and 78 of the Copyright, Designs and Patents Act 1988.

First Published in 2021

ISBN 978-1-914366-80-2 (Paperback)

Book cover design and Book layout by:
>White Magic Studios
>www.whitemagicstudios.co.uk

Published by:
>Maple Publishers
>1 Brunel Way,
>Slough,
>SL1 1FQ, UK
>www.maplepublishers.com

A CIP catalogue record for this title is available from the British Library.

All rights reserved. No part of this book may be reproduced or translated by any form or by any means, electronic or mechanical, including photocopying, recording or by any information storage and retrieval system without written permission from the author.

The views expressed in this work are solely those of the author and do not necessarily reflect the views of the publisher, and the publisher hereby disclaims any responsibility for them.

CONTENTS

Chapter 1: Four Types of People 5

Chapter 2: Building Trust 14

Chapter 3: Inspiring Trust 19

Chapter 4: The 15 Behaviours of EQ 34

Chapter 5: 4 Ts of Change 52

Chapter 6: Blue Chair, Pink Chair 58

Chapter 7: 10 Reasons Why Top Talent Will Leave 65

Chapter 8: Diversity in Full 67

Chapter 9: The 5 Ws and 1 H 73

Chapter 10: Smarta Objectives 76

Chapter 11: Sharing Factual Knowledge 78

Chapter 12: The 3 Ws and WIN 81

Chapter 13: The 12th Man – A WADES 87

Chapter 14: Free Gifts 98

Chapter 15: Scouting Player 104

Chapter 16: My Philosophy 109

Introduction

I would like to take this opportunity to thank you for taking out time to read my book and I hope it gives you plenty to think about. You will learn some great tools and techniques to help develop your coaching and in general, become a better person.

My football journey began over 35 years ago as a young lad and was very lucky to have to parents (Eddie & Bea) who made sure their sons (Jason (me) and my brother Eddie Jr) played sports and one of which was football. My dad was a very good player and as most keen dads do, he started coaching the teams, so I was always out playing football.

I've been around sports all my life and added the skills of emotional intelligence, so I could understand a wide range of behaviours in business and sports. I've taken many qualifications in business and sports to be able to coach players at the level I do.

I was born in New Zealand and in the 70s moved to the United Kingdom (Coventry) where I lived since the move and married the true love of my life Carly, who gave me two wonderful sons Joshua and Alfie.

I've managed and coached teams from under 8s all the way up to non-league. I've talked about EQ in business and worked with young sportsmen around the 15 behaviours. I would also like to thank all the people who have helped me on my journey – far too many to list here, but they know who they are.

Please enjoy the book and if you have any questions, please drop me an email at jasonpyott@gmail.com.

Chapter 1: Four Types of People

I thought this would be a great place to start the book. As coaches we have different types of people to deal with, from players to parents to fans. The diagram showing four types of people will give you a deeper understanding of how your group will learn and best methods for progressing them the pitfalls of having too many from one of the four types and if so, how you deal with this.

So, what do I mean by "four types of people"?

Let's go through the different sections to putting your team into the right area so that we as coaches have a quick and deeper understanding on how these players will learn quicker and more effective.

The diagram 1 below shows the four countries we will be using for this exercise.

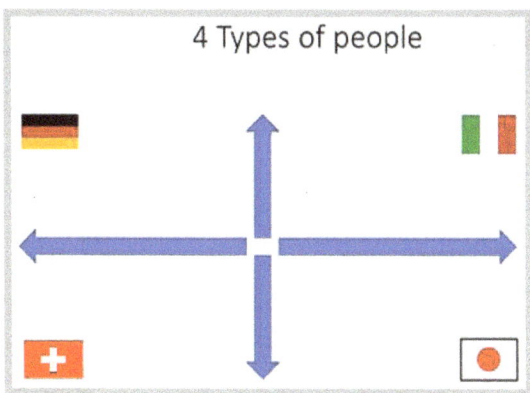

Countries denoting Four Types of People

As you see, we will use Germany, Italy, Switzerland, and Japan as the four types of people. This will become clearer as you move through the process.

The second part will give you a choice and you can do this yourself, so you know what type of person you are first.

You must decide if you are **outgoing** or **reserved** as a person.

Reserved is someone who is slow to reveal emotions or opinions.

Outgoing is someone who is friendly and energetic.

So, which one are you? I will use myself as an example as we go along; so you can see how we will fill it out and understand what it means.

I'm a very outgoing person, so I now know that I will either be a German or Italian as the outgoing arrow is going up as seen in Diagram 2 below.

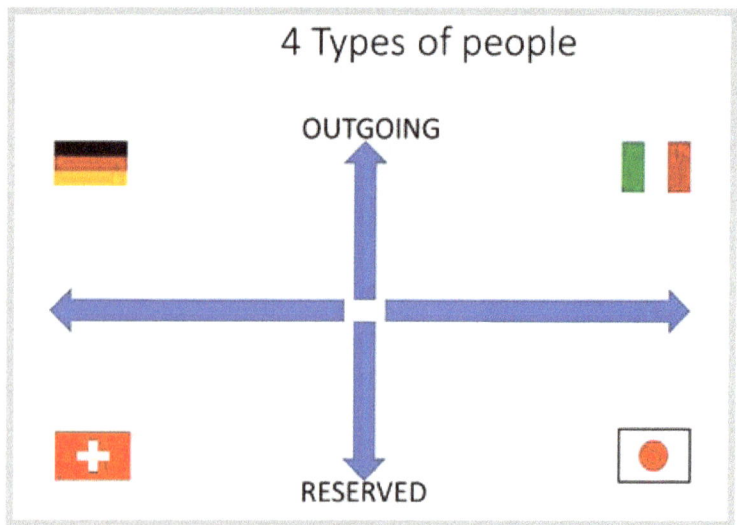

Outgoing and Reserved People

The next step is to understand if I'm Task orientated, or People orientated. The Diagram 3 below shows Task on the left and People on the right.

Task-oriented person is someone who likes doing the piece of work, especially one that is done regularly.

People-oriented person is someone who enjoys or is particularly good at interacting with others.

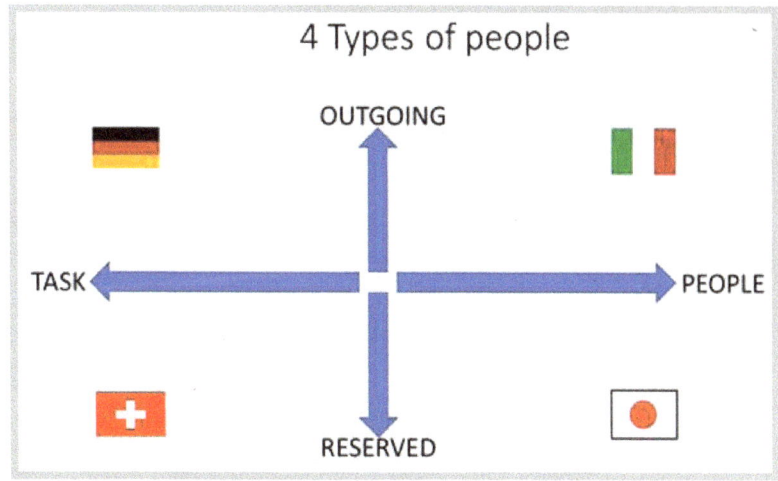

Task-oriented and People Oriented

We now know that I'm outgoing and I'm very people-focused. So this makes me an Italian for the purpose of this exercise. If you don't have any info about what it means, refer to the diagram below showing where you fit into the four types of people and what each type of persons characteristics are.

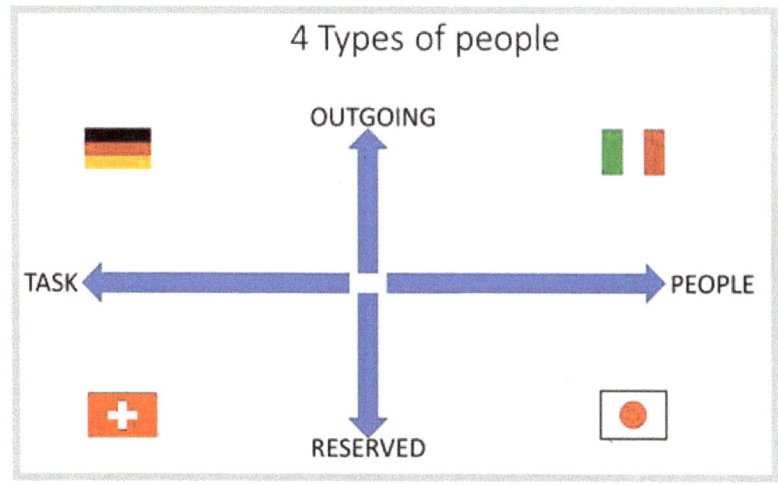

Knowing where we fit

Let's look at the characteristics of the four types of people and see if these fit where you put yourself.

German: **(DIRECT)** Fast, loud, talks more than listens and states more than asks, big gestures-points, forceful and challenging.

Italy: (**INTERACTIVE**) Fast, loud, talks more than listens and tells stories also talks with hands, dramatic and energetic.

Switzerland: (**CAUTIOUS**) Slow, soft, listens more than talks and asks penetrating questions, few controlled gestures, clarifying and monotone.

Japan: (**STEADY**) Slow, soft, listens more than talks and asks more than states with gentle reassuring gestures, conversational and warm.

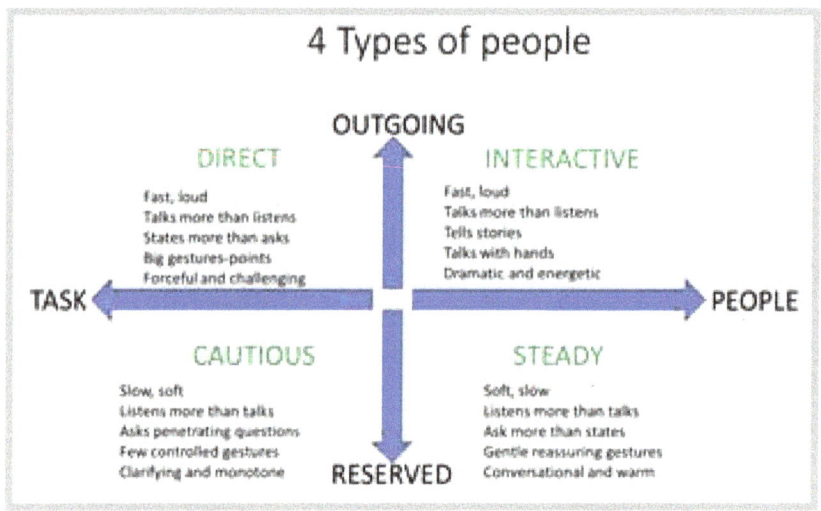

Characteristics of Four Types of People

We now know the meaning behind each of the four countries and understand the characteristics they possess. So, where did you put yourself and does it fit?

Now think about your players, go through the exercise, and place them in the correct country. It is very interesting to do this with the players as it gives you a chance to see what type of person they are and if you are on the same wave length as them. So I hear you asking, "Great, I know where they fit in the diagram but how does that help me when I coach them?"

To begin, allow me to tell you about a school in Bromsgrove (UK) where I go every year to teach emotional intelligence (for free), and it is fantastic for kids aged 13/14 and with mixed abilities."?

Big thanks to Steve Swaffield, a great mate (German type, outgoing, task) and his school for inviting me every year.

During the day, I have four classes of children (mixed boys and girls) for 60 minutes each. Each class has 24 children.

I did this exercise with the teachers and children to put them in the correct country for each class.

Class 1: Germany 4, Italy 16, Switzerland 4, Japan 0.

Class 2: Germany 10, Italy, 3, Switzerland 10, Japan 1.

Class 3: Germany 8, Italy 7, Switzerland 7, Japan 2.

Class 4: Germany 3, Italy 18, Switzerland 2, Japan 1.

Now, the first class was an eye opener. The first thing I noticed that was the teacher looked drained and was struggling to keep the students under control and you ask why? Well, I can tell you why you get this many Italians in a group. It's party time as they have so much energy that the group is bubbling but on the down side it makes it very hard to learn as concentration span is not a strong point.

Just think about the old saying **opposites attract** and look at the diagram of 4 types of people. Think of the people at work or at the football field with whom you have great relationships and those with whom you have just relationships. I know that if I'm with other Italian country types then we have a great time, but after a while we start getting on each other's nerves. Take a minute and think about it. The types of people that I have great relationships are from the other three countries.

Let's look at class three. You guessed it was a pleasure to educate them and we got through so much more as the group was very balanced. I'm not saying to pick your team based on four types of people but once you understand the types of people you have, you can plan the best type of learning for them, both as a group and individuals.

I hope you have a clear understanding of the types of players in your team now. We will look at different types of methods of coaching and mentoring them.

Let's look at the FA's five of coaching methods and see where they fit into the four types of people. Look at the table below. Think about what you would use on the different types of players and what you wouldn't.

Coaching Methodology	Command	Question and Answer	Observation and Feedback	Guided Discovery	Trial and error
Player/Coach Interventions	Coach tells and shows required solution	Coach leads with question to gain response from players.	Coach and players observe.	Coach asks a question or issues a challenge.	Players and/ or coach decide on the challenge.
Example	"I want you to…"	"What do you think…"	"Let's watch this…"	"Can you show me …"	"Try this for yourself …"
Description	Coach tells, explains and shows how to do something.	Coach poses questions and players offer verbal solution to the challenge.	Coach and players observe and discuss feedback.	Coach challenges and players offer visual demonstration of possible solution.	Players are encouraged to find solution with minimal support from coach.

The 5 methods of coaching

Remember the four types of people.

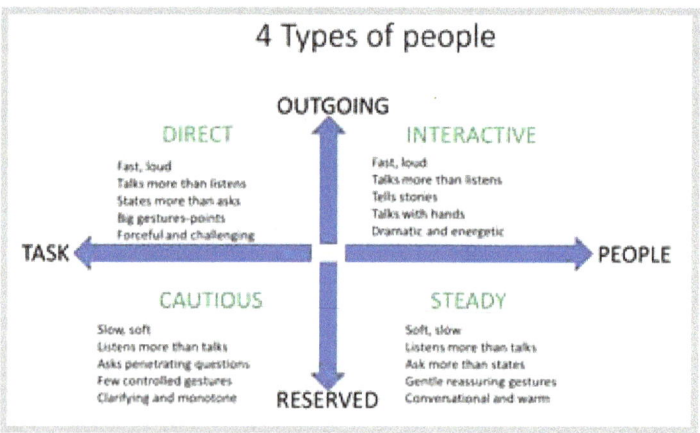

GERMAN

Now, let's start with the German type of people at top left. Direct is the main header. If we start at **command** and work our way through the five coaching methods, we can see that these people are direct and fast, loud and so on. So yes, it would be a very strong method of coaching to use "I want you to". Make it very direct and short as they want to get on with it, and use the hands and voice for big gestures. **Question and answer** can work but you will find that the German people want to be told and get on with it. So when you use this method, don't ask too many questions as they just want to get on with it. **Observation and feedback** can cause the German type of person to lose concentration very quickly as they prefer to perform than watch but again, if done at right time and for a short period of time, it can be successful. **Guided**

discovery can work well with the German type as the coach issues a challenge. This is direct and challenging, so a very good way to get them learning is to conduct reviews in small groups, so they can show you what they have from the challenge and get back to practice. **Trial and error** works well for the German types as they get instruction, go off, and practice it just keeping it short and when you need to step in to help be direct. Show them what you want and how you want it to be. Just keep it short.

ITALY

Now let's look at the Italy type on the top right. Interactive is the main header, so if we look at **command**, "I want you to" doesn't go down well with them as it is very direct. They want to spend more time discussing the "how" and in most cases everything else going on. If you do choose to use the Italians, take a bit more time on your command so they understand and focus on it. **Question and answers** is what they love as it lets them to get involved and give their points of view on the question.. Asking "What do you think" will get them going on overdrive, so remember the other types of people in the team and how they will feel. If you can set the question up where they are together then stop and ask away. Just remember they will stand and talk stories with you all day and get that ball rolling! **Observation and feedback** is another great method for the Italian types as they will tell you what they see all day if given the chance. They will not only respond to "Let's watch this" but they will tell you all the examples and this may lead to losing focus on what they should be watching. **Guided discovery** can work well but you need to keep control as if a few Italians get together watching and then showing can be a little time consuming and gets a little lost. So as a coach this can work but will require a constant focus on your behalf. Finally, **Trial and error** doesn't always work well for the Italians as they would stop if they don't get it and want to see it again. They don't always want to work it out when they can be shown it again and have another go.

SWITZERLAND

Let's look at the Swiss type on the bottom left, cautious is the main header. Let's start with the **command.** This works but only in big, mixed-type groups of people as they love the telling and showing side but don't like it loud and fast. Make sure you give them the data (show and tell) in the command and they will be happy. **Questions and answers** is for the swiss type of person who loves information and data. The more they can take in, the more it becomes better. So answer is more important than question as they need to know the how or why, when asking questions to them. If they know the answer they will talk about it all day but if they don't, don't duel on the question. They will want the answer straight away. **Observation and feedback** is a style that that the Swiss types love as they love to watch how it is done (visual data) and in a group feedback session you will see a lot of passion as once they understand how it works or if it has gone wrong, they will use that data to solve the issues. **Guided discovery** needs focus as we know how cautious the Swiss type of person can be. So make the challenge achievable or when the Swiss have something new they can close up. For **Trial and error**, we know the Swiss type of person can ask questions, so make sure you explain how important it is that they don't have to get it right first time (error side) as it is good to put them in an area they don't choose to go to normally but not where they lose interest and get frustrated.

JAPAN

The Japanese type of people on the bottom right are by far the fewest in any group. Just think they are people-focused and reserved which when you think about doesn't seem to go together and has a main header of Steady. When we look at **command**, they find it difficult to relate to as command can go well with loud and fast and they like things to be in a very steady and slower pace and with this style of coaching they might not raise a question if they are scared of the direct approach they might receive. This doesn't mean they will not listen to the command but you will have to struggle to get the best out of them. Considering **Questions and answers**, the Japanese type of person likes the question side but will ask a lot of questions about the question and not talk about the answer. So make sure you don't let this drift them away from the answer you want. **Observation and feedback** is a very good style to use for the Japanese as they like to watch and take their time to talk about it in a group and come up with **feedback**. Make sure they are given the time and don't rush. Keep it steady. **Guided discovery** is another steady way to help to coach the Japanese type of people as it gives them a challenge in a group and they will be a big part as they will ask a lot of questions around the challenge. **Trial and error** needs a lot of focus from the coach as the Japanese type of person can stop and ask a lot of questions on every part. So make sure you tell them how important and ok it is to make errors and how they need to make sure they do it at a speed they can cope with STEADY.

So, as you can see there is a lot to consider when it comes to the type of people in your team and what type of coaching style to use, but I think we can agree that one type does not fit all.

On another note, you can use this to work out the type of person the parents are very quickly and understand what they think they need to keep them happy; German type of person be direct and use main header from diagram to use correct style for the other three types of person.

The more you practice this and build it into your sessions, you will find the sessions flowing much better, but it takes time so prepare and practice.

Chapter 2: Building Trust

"Trust" is a word we hear all the time, but do we really know how we trust someone or why they trust you? I have designed a formula that will this

First, take a few minutes and write down the names of 5 people who you trust.

Now, write down why you think you trust them, look for as many words that describe them.

Now, think about the 5 people you do not trust and write down as many words that describe them.

So, let's look at the formula for trust.

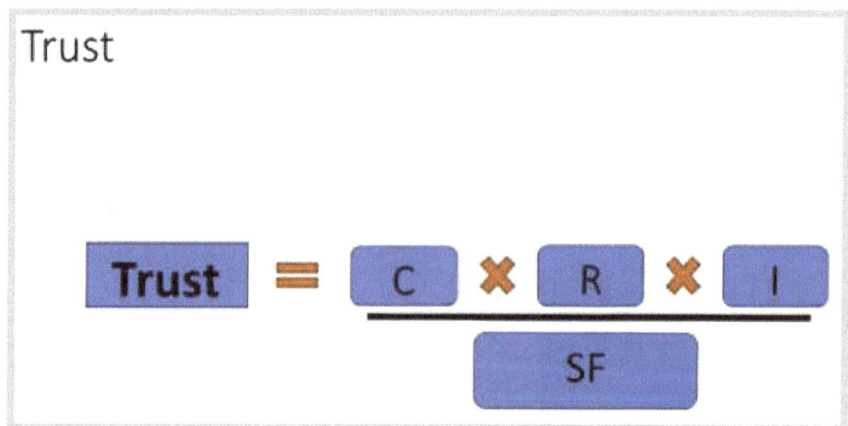

Above is the formula for trust and you can see that Trust equals C x R x I divided by SF.

Now, take a few minutes to check what words you put down in the previous exercise and see if any words start with the letters C, R, I, SF.

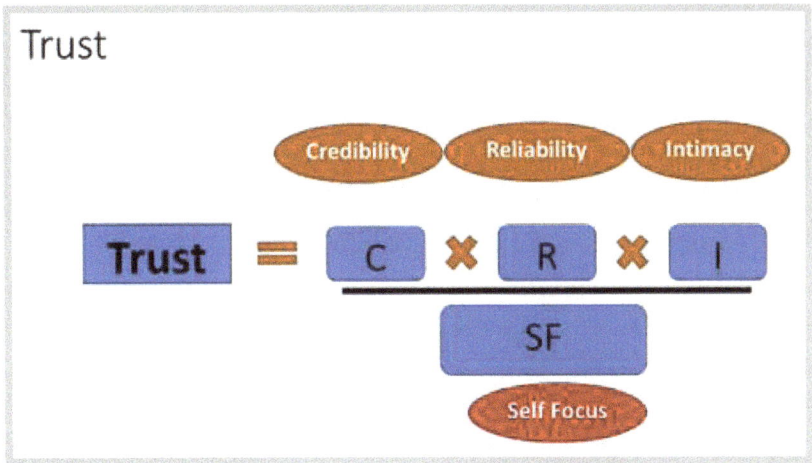

The C is Credibility.

The R is Reliability.

The I is Intimacy.

The SF is Self-Focus.

Credibility is the quality of being trusted and believed in. The people we trust will be people who come across as creditable to us. Maybe a player or a coach who has done something we are happy with or completed the task on their own. Go back to your list, look at the names, and see if you find them creditable.

Reliability is the quality of being trustworthy or performing consistently well. Think about the players who have a good game say 7 or 8 every game and who know how to play the way you have coached. You will find in the training sessions that these people are the ones you would leave to their own devices as they are more consistent and can manage themselves much more often than others. Another part is behaviour and you trust them to behave when giving a task to do.

Intimacy resembles close friendships and when we look at it from a football perspective then it's all about sharing knowledge and listening to that person in return when they share knowledge.

Self-Focus is the conscious attention on oneself and one's thoughts, needs, desires, and emotions. The old saying "it's all about me" is when we have high self-focus. We all know the people at the back of the room or in a group that never speak which is low self-focus.

Now, we need to learn about three more concepts to complete the formula – brand, presence and sharing

Brand is your identity. If you look at say a company like McDonalds, they don't have the best burgers in the city you live. But they are good, very well priced, and the service is quick. If I ask "could I get a better burger?", the answer would be "yes". But do I get all the other benefits? No. If you see the golden archers in the sky, you know what it is and don't forget the slogan "I'm loving it".

Presence is the state of existing, occurring, or being present. Being always there for the players is a good example and when you add reliability, it will strengthen up why you trust that person or business. It is the fact that someone or something is in place.

Sharing is to have a portion of something with another or others. So in coaching, when we set up a session, we are sharing the knowledge we have.

We learnt the types of people and the style of managing them. Now, we are on our way to build trust with the players and even the parents of the players as the players talk to their parents."?

Now, we have one more part to show to complete the formula, brand, presence, and sharing.

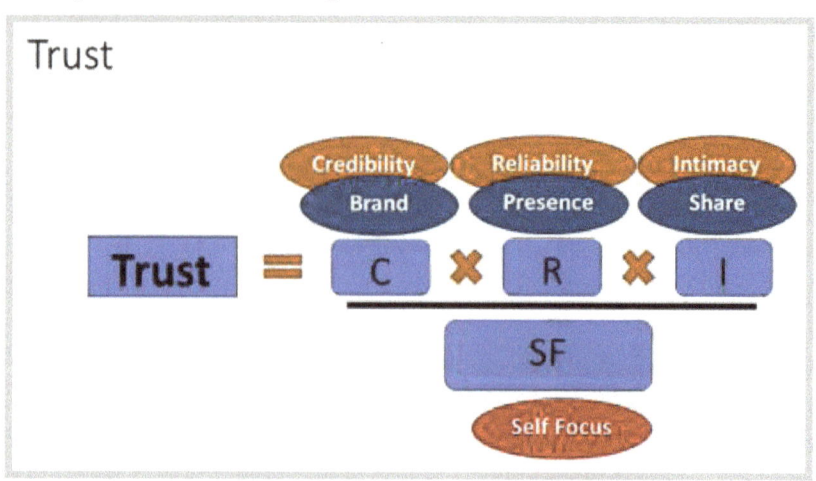

When looking at yourself, players, and the team, think about how other people see these three areas. Let's consider yourself and think about what is my brand, presence, and how do I share my knowledge.

Look at the formula below and write down what you think your brand is, your presence is, and how you share your knowledge with your players.

Now that we have understood the formula and what it means to build trust, we can do a little exercise to know where we are on trust.

I want you to rate yourself out of 10, 1 being lowest and 10 being highest on each of the four factors credibility, reliability, intimacy, and self-focus. Once you give yourself a score on these four, you need to calculate credibility x reliability x intimacy and write down the answer. Once you have this number, divide it by your self-focus score.

We will use the formula below to look at this person and see how trust worthy they are.

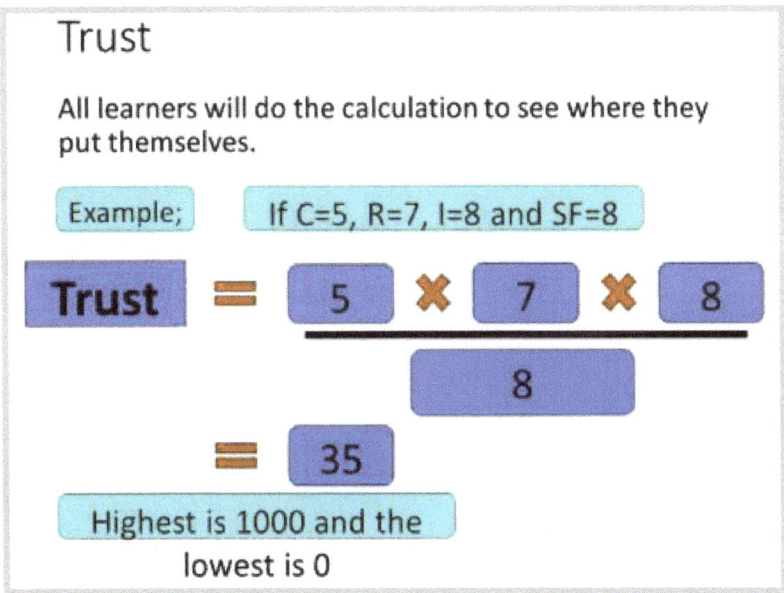

As you can see, the person in this example is in between for credibility and this is a steady score. But I believe they do not always tell the truth or are not believed when they tell people how or what to do. But looking at the reliability score of 7, when they say they will do something, they normally do it. So there is a strong part of trust and last but not the least, on the top line we have a score of 8 for intimacy, which you would hope a coach would think when they need to share information and knowledge with the players. We just need to make sure that information is correct and has a good impact on the players.

Now, let's consider the self-focus score of 8 which is high and this person likes to be the centre of attention. The problem is if you start hitting 9s and 10s, none of your players will matter as it will be "look at me" style and "how did I do" and this would drive the focus away from your players and as a coach you should focus on the team and not yourself

Now, for self-focus if you are scoring a 1 or 2, this also creates problems, as you will struggle to get across your points and knowledge. As an example in work you consider the person who just gets on with their job and when it comes to promotion they always get over looked. Imagine having a coach with a score of 9 and a player with a score of 2, I tell you the coach won't even know they are there.

Think about how you can use these areas to improve coaching and the ways that you could impact the session, so the players truly trust you and learn at the highest level. But also how you can get them to understand what is needed for them to grow trust with you. An example game can be a blind fold test where the players blind fold one of the player from the team and you put 3 players on either side, and ask them to lean back and fall over whilst the 6 players. Now ask them to link each other's arms and catch the blind folded player. watch to see the ones who lean full back and trust the players that hold them then put a couple of the more lively lads as holders and one of the less lively ones in blind fold. You will see them look behind as they don't trust the players hold the link.

For credibility, ask each player to tell a story about something they did for team's good and then ask another player to tell a story about when the player who has just told a story about himself did something good.

Intimacy can be shown in so many different ways. One such exercise is making small groups and ask each player to share something on a subject you give them like about our club.

Chapter 3: Inspiring Trust

We have learnt about building trust in the previous chapter. This chapter will give you some techniques to use for inspiring trust in your coaching role and everyday life.

We will look at the 7 areas of inspiring trust:

Why perception kills?

Frames of reference

Rapport

Listening

Dealing with conflict

Openness

Reframing

Why perception kills?

Our beliefs are limited to what we know or have been taught, and can extend up to what we hear from other people. If we trust them, we will mostly believe in what we are told

Below is the perception pyramid:

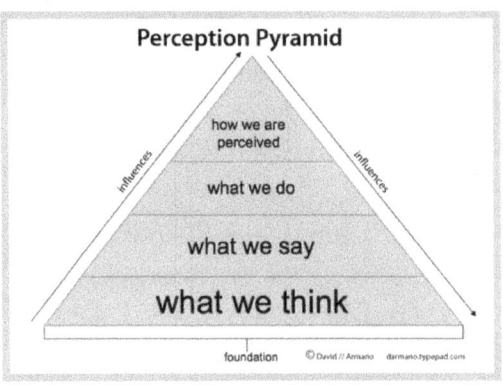

As you can see, the sequence is *what we think*, leading to *what we say*, and *what we do* which will lead to *how we are perceived*.

You might trust someone because they are creditable, reliable, and share knowledge with you. But what if they gave you the wrong information and you believed it to be true? When we ask football coaches, we will hear many different beliefs. I'm not saying one coach's beliefs are better than another's, but when we want the correct information for example, one coach tells you that a player is left-footed and the other coach tells you the same player is right-footed then one of the best techniques is to "go and see", and make your own decision as you trust both the coaches but have different information.

Self-regard plays a big part in trust and perception. A great example is the X factor where people come to the show and tell the judges that they are the next big thing in music for them to start signing and then all of us cringe for them when they start singing. When we talk about self-regard, it is defined as a high level as we really believe in ourselves but when we talk about emotional intelligence, we call this a cost of high and it can be as bad as having a low self-regard in some cases even worse.

Think about when a parent calls you to ask, "Can my child come for training?". Then they chat about the ability of their child and what they have done, and you get very excited and can't wait to see them. When the day arrives, you are shocked to see the child cannot pass the ball or shows a low level of technique. This can be very hard to manage as the child and the parent both have totally different beliefs.

I say it's a bit like a cat looking in a mirror and seeing a lion.

How do you start to manage this? The best policy is to be honest. In the next part, we will talk about different styles to use covert or overt. The best way for training is to talk to the parent and child both and make the parents see the child's performance as they are the only people who can truly see this and hopefully they understand where their child is and bring down their self-regard to a better balance. This will help the child try harder and learn quicker.

I hear a lot of coaches saying they have a huge confidence as a person but we must make sure it's not a cost of high . Being confident and not completing a task means we, as coaches, need to work to bring down the self-regard in a controlled manner, just like how you would train a child who showed low self-regard. We tend to look at this more as it stands out especially if you have a team full of Italians from the four types of people.

So, remember to "go see" or take the child through the "go see" once they see it, they will believe it.

What do you see below? Are the lines horizontal, parallel, or do they slope?

Are the horizontal lines parallel or do they slope?

What you see still can be confusing as the picture above can trick the mind to think it is something else. This is where the coach comes into picture. He can ask the child their thoughts on the "go see" and give the child a deeper understanding. and hopefully get them to tell them what they need them to understand. Once the child gives this information, you can move forward and help in not only improving the technical side of their game but also the emotional intelligence side on how to understand and control their emotions.

Frames of reference

What does this mean to coaches? The human brain considers the familiar aspects as positive and the unfamiliar as negative. You grow up speaking certain languages, wearing particular clothes, and holding defined beliefs or values. You consider what you speak, wear and hold good. Other people grow up speaking other languages, wearing other types of clothing, and having other beliefs. You consider these negative.

When you begin a relationship with a child, start from the place of overlap between you and the child in order to build trust.

Child

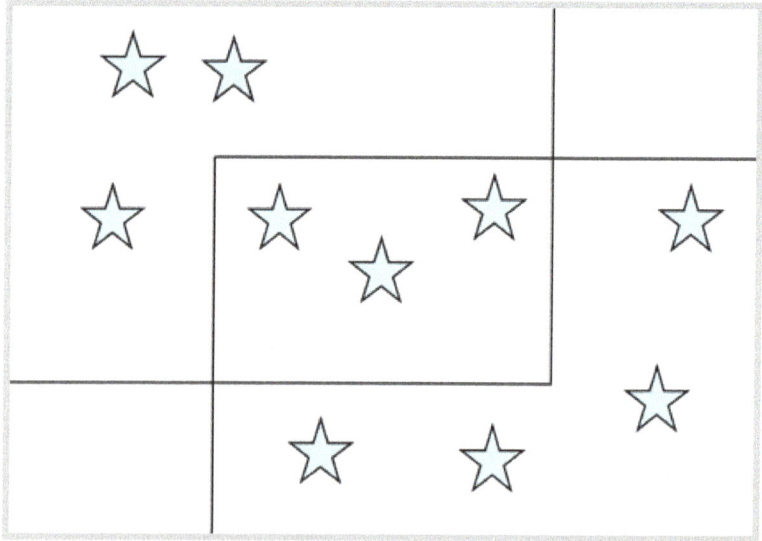

Coach

Find the common ground between you and the child. In business, this might need a bit research but as a football coach you will have football as the overlap to find out what they like about the game and even who they support. This will start a steady relationship and if the beliefs are different, it will allow you both to talk about those areas, as you have started to build a real trust through your frames of reference.

When we start the journey of coaching, no one would think how far you need to go to become a better coach. I always thought I knew football better but day by day I'm learning how to make myself better and by understanding your players and their parents from the start, you will grow better and stronger relationships all round.

Find the overlaps and start to grow the relationship. Be open minded to beliefs that are not the same as yours, try and understand their points of view. You might even learn something new. If you still don't agree then share your views and respect theirs too.

Rapport

Rapport has three areas – body language, tone, and words.

But do you know in what percentage is body, tone, or words present in a typical conversation.

Write down your answers and at the end I will put the results.

Body?

Tone?

Words?

Let's take a look at "body" and start to get you thinking as a coach. If you are using **command** as a way to coach, let the player know the way you want it done and decide to talk to this player. If using a command, do you think charging over and standing right in front of the players while waving your arms around will help or standing back and keeping your arm movements down would be more effective (still in a command approach)? Remember as coaches what we pick up from our players and their body gives us so much to see on how they feel and what they think.

Now we will look at "tone". Again using the same **command** style you decide to tell the player what you want and start to shout out the instructions in a commanding style, how will the player feel? Think about being assertive with your voice but in a controlled manner. Talk clearly and to the point. Remember the four types of people? Yes? Great then make sure you know them as a person and the style they prefer.

Finally let's look at the "words". It is important to choose the right words to say and also in the right way. Sometimes, we see the players losing interest after a while and start thinking about what they are having for tea.

Now that you have written down you answers and know a little bit about the three areas of rapport, we will see the facts. If you want to change the answers, now is the time.

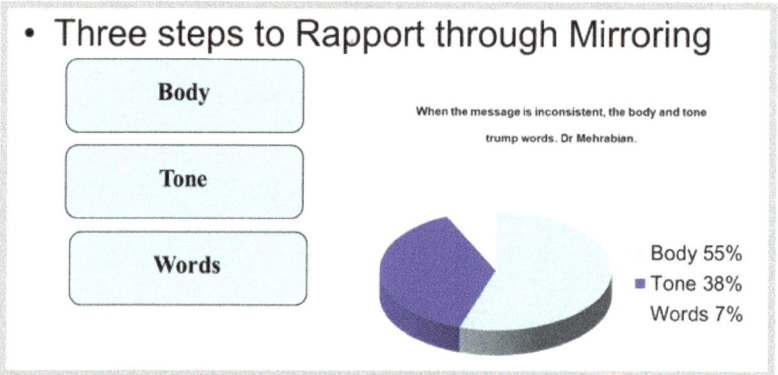

As seen in the above diagram, Body is 55% of the conversation, tone is 38%, and words cover only 7%.

Now, think about the coaching situations you have been in and recall how they went. Write down two or three of the situations and see what part was most important. If you have recorded sessions then watch them from a body-tone-words perspective. You will see it's not so much about the words as it is how they come across.

Example:

You have to tell a player to stop messing around and the words are "can you please focus on the drill and stop messing around"

Now, the same words can be said in a different body language and tone as in the two following examples:

Example 1: You run over waving your arms and your tone is very loud and aggressive

Example 2: You walk over stop 10 feet away and with a smile on your face and your tone is calm and clear.

Watching coaching videos online will not only give you some great sessions but also help you understand how to deliver the information to the players. Great coaches know how to get the best out of their players as they understand the type of people they are. But more importantly they also understand the style that the players prefer to be coached and with the correct body language, tone, and words, this makes up for a complete coaching.

Great coaches will mirror the players when delivering drills and technical points. Some don't even know they are doing it as it has been years of perfecting the way they want to be seen as a coach with strong beliefs and philosophies.

Listening

Now, this one is very interesting as we all think we listen well, but do we really?

Below is a simple but very effective way to help people understand how important it truly is to listen, and block all those other noises around them.

We define "listening" as giving attention to someone or something in order to hear them.

So, the word is to listen first evaluate later

The five steps to listening

1. Temporarily suspend your agenda
2. Attend the speaker
3. Clarify and amplify the speaker's words
4. Reflect the content
5. Acknowledge the emotions

> Pretend you are a mirror. When you listen, you are there to reflect a person's words and emotions

Step 1: Temporarily suspend your agenda

What do we mean by this? Well, it is straight forward! You're going to hear them without asking what it is about and also not thinking about what it is you want to get across. You will have to wait for your turn to speak.

Step 2: Attend the speaker

Give your full attention to the speaker. Make sure you face them and have strong eye contact and body tone.

Step 3: Clarify and amplify the speaker's words

This means don't be afraid to ask and repeat the questions when you don't understand any of the points. So they get to hear them when important part of the conversation and use different tones for how you want them to hear your replies.

Step 4: Reflect the content

This simply means to take on board what has been said, take time to understand and put together your reply in a factful way.

Step 5: Acknowledge the emotions

Let the person know you feel and understand them the way they come across as the sincerer as you are. Then they will open up more.

Below is a simple activity for you to do with the players and even parents it can be a lot of fun as well.

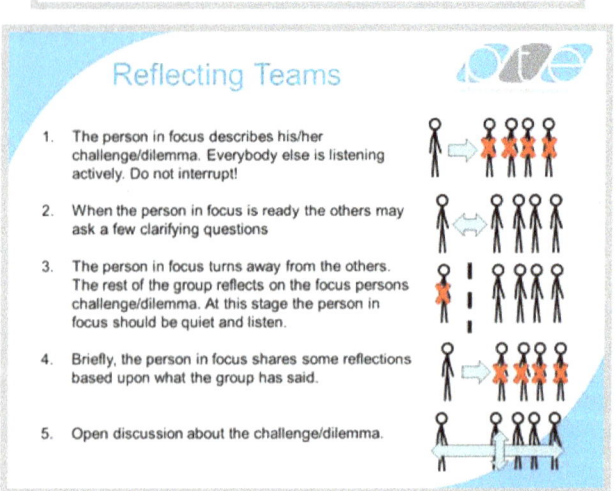

Step 1: We get a person to share a challenge or dilemma with a group. No one in the group can speak and the group must face the person speaking.

Step 2: The people who have been listening ask a few selective questions to the person with the challenge or dilemma.

Step 3: The person who had the challenge or dilemma now turns away and listens to the group reflecting what they have heard. You will get a clear focus by turning away your goal will be to not just listen but understand what is being said.

Step 4: The person who shared the challenge or dilemma now asks questions about what they have just heard from the group.

Step 5: Conclude with an open discussion with everyone talking about the challenge or dilemma. Trust me, this works so well. If every one of you get into a deep conversation with me and I turn my back, don't worry. Lol!

Major points to listening are to stop and hear what is being said and drop your agenda until you hear the other person, and this will allow you to get a deeper understanding and by reflecting make better decisions.

Remember

We listen to get information, learn, understand, and enjoy ourselves. It's impossible to hear what someone else is communicating if we are talking or if we have some preloaded thoughts or information, the learning, or the understanding someone else wants to give us. We must let go all of our desires to talk, relate, and understand their words in our way. It is not easy; it takes practice and constant reminding to listen well.

Dealing with Conflicts

This is a subject that they don't warn you about as a coach (lol) and trust me, it can take up most of your time if you allow it to. I hear you saying but how do I not allow it then.

I will use the two brothers Covert and Overt. These boys are very different in how they behave.

Covert approaches the covert/passive, aggressive person gently and firmly. I hear you saying, "How can I be gentle and firm?" It's simple. Use a soft-voice approach but what you say needs to be firm like "stop that now" which is very direct and to the point. As with covert, you listen and then assert.

Overt is a different brother. If you expect bad behaviour to disappear because you ignore that it fuels resentment, backstabbing and ultimately sabotage, and with these types of people, you listen first, let them come down from the high and then approach calm and to the point.

A good example is if I am going out with the lads and said that I would be back home by 9 pm but I get in at 12 pm, the good lady starts going on. The best thing to do is just keep quiet and let it run down. Trust me, I have been in this situation a few times in early days.

So again, as the coach, we will not always have happy players or parents as all we can do is be transparent with our philosophy and direction, and fear about how we deliver results. But understand the type of person you are dealing with, as finding if they are covert or overt can help you handle them in a much better way.

If you feel the conflict is too big and you need to push it up the ladder, then don't hesitate as most clubs have a welfare office and a chairman. They are not only there for the players but for the staff as well. If it gets too hard, make sure after you take notes and reflect the outcome as not all outcomes suit both parties but remember if honest and clear you will sleep well at night.

Read club's handbook and if needed take advice of the FA or other governing body.

Openness

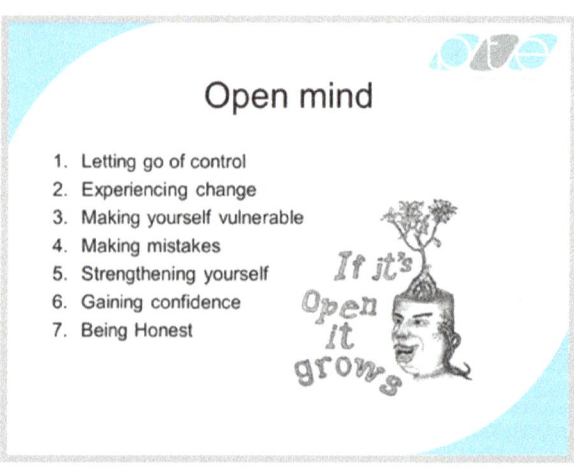

1. Letting go of control. When you open your mind, you free yourself from having to be in complete control of your thoughts. You allow yourself to experience new ideas and thoughts and you challenge the beliefs you currently have. It can be very liberating to look at the world through an open mind.

2. Experiencing changes. Opening up your mind to new ideas allows you to the opportunity to change what you think about and how you view the world. Now, this doesn't mean you necessarily will change your beliefs, but you have the option to do so, when you think with an open mind.

3. Making yourself vulnerable. One of the scariest (and greatest) things about seeing the world through an open mind is making yourself vulnerable. In agreeing to have an open-minded view of the world, you're admitting you don't know everything and that there are possibilities you may not have considered. This vulnerability can be both terrifying and exhilarating.

4. Making mistakes. Making mistakes doesn't seem like it would be much of a benefit, but it truly is. When you open your mind and allow yourself to see things from others' perspectives, you allow yourself not only to recognize the potential mistakes you've made, but also to make new mistakes. Doesn't sound like much fun, but it's a great thing to fall and get back up again.

5. Strengthening yourself. Open-mindedness provides a platform on which you can build ideas, piling one idea on top of another. With an open mind you can learn about new things and you can use the new ideas to build on the old ideas. Everything you experience can add up, strengthening who you are and what you believe in. It's very hard to build on experiences without an open mind.

6. Gaining confidence. When you live with an open mind, you have a strong sense of self. You are not confined by your own beliefs, nor are you confined by the beliefs of others. For that reason, you are able to have and gain confidence as you learn more and more about the world around you. Open-mindedness helps you to learn and grow, strengthening your belief in yourself.

7. Being honest. There is an honesty that comes with an open mind because being open-minded means admitting that you aren't an all-knowing person. It means believing that whatever truth you find might always have more to it than you realize. This understanding creates an underlying sense of honesty that permeates the character of anyone who lives with an open mind.

Fixed mindset VS Open Growth mindset

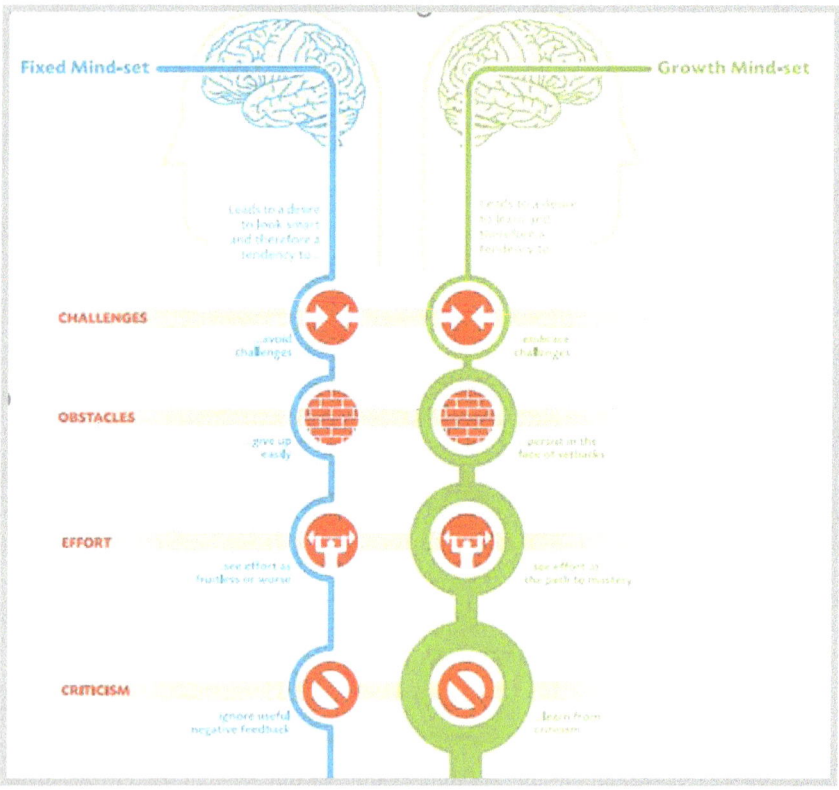

If I can give you a piece of advice, then openness would be the area not to turn a blind eye to, as no one can come back to you if you follow these simple steps and apply them in your everyday life.

If you like to be in control then that's fine but learn when you can let it go, as we say in football terms guide and you will discover when it is important to take control but give the player a chance to lead control as this will develop not only the players but also you as a coach. Experiencing change and a lot of coaches think this has to work but some of the best change I experienced have not worked but they give you the platform to work on the change and adjust how you need to work for yourself and your players.

Formations are a great way to look at the changes and they also position how many defenders who had a go at other positions and strikers who went into defense. This better allows players to see and feel what it's all about than to put this into words. People have been asking me over the years if getting tattoos hurt and my answer always was what hurts me might not hurt you or it might. So the only way to find out is to get a tattoo. This is where parents, players, and coaches need to be open minded.

Making mistakes is a very frustrating experience at times but trust me without it we never learn and understand the difficulty of a problematic situation. Some of the best mistakes I have made, have made me the coach I am today. Yes, there are some I would not like repeat again but that is a learning process. There are some mistakes that I have repeated several times again and again as the reward out ways the risk and never be scared to say I got it wrong as I remember the time when I was playing cricket in South Africa and nicked one to the keeper but the umpire said, "Not out!" and they went crazy calling me by all those names and one of them asked "what did that hit" I replied "my bat". All of a sudden they didn't know what to say.

Again, explain the "why you did it" and the risk and rewards as when people understand the 4 T's of change they will see you in a different light. Look for the people to learn from as if you can speed up your learning from those who have made similar mistakes or the ones you haven't even come across yet they listen and learn to find a mentor. These are not always top-level coaches. They could be in your grass root clubs. Never overlook that area experience comes with time but you can speed it up.

When looking at helping goalkeepers, I like to go to striker coaching to see how these players are learning, so we can work on stopping this and the other way around for strikers.

Other sports are a great way to strengthen your coaching and learning if they are done in a different or even a better way. We can apply this into our training and coaching.

As coaches, we don't spend enough time celebrating success as most of us don't know what success looks like and this took me a long time to get as we look at success on winning and trophies. But I can tell you that success for me is one -building great people, two - making myself a better person, and three - enjoying what I do.

Think about you giving up your time no matter where you are in your coaching journey, so this is a success straight away. Take time to reflect on this and every time I see a person achieving an outcome on a challenge, this is a success. So stop and catch these points as they are the reason we do it. To win is nice and I'm as driven as the next person but knowing your environment will allow you to push yourself for different types of success. If you are a top-flight coach or a manager then results are important. But they are the outcome of the input so make sure you understand your inputs and celebrate when they go right.

The last part is being honest and what I mean is to be honest with yourself and with others.

The news you give at times is hard as you might leave someone's pride and joy out of the team but let them know the "why" and "what" your decision was based on as people might not like the news but will respect it for your honesty. The easiest way to be honest is to try and use facts where you can, as we all have an opinion but this shouldn't matter but the facts will. Take it that the player has missed four training sessions and you put him out the team. His parent comes and asks the reason and also tells you that he is the leading goal scorer, which is a true fact. But you've already informed the player at the beginning that if players miss training they will start on the bench and this is also a fact. All the players and parents will respect you and go forward with your decisions.

Reframing

So, what is this? Trust me this has got me out of a lot of concerns in sport and business.

To reframe something is to put it in a different setting, context, or frame. When you do so, the meaning of the experience or the object changes. When the meaning changes, the response and behaviour changes too.

There are two types of reframing: content and context.

To reframe well ask, "In what context would x (a negative) have a positive value?" For content ask, "what else could this mean?" or "how could it be positive?"

Business

Example: Manufacturing of the product and delivery will be delayed (negative) because R&D caught a flaw in the design (negative).

Reframe: Thanks to R&D catching a fatal flaw (positive), we've made the aircraft more robust (positive). The delay in manufacturing and delivery serves a bigger and better purpose.

Sport

Example: We could not play the game today (negative) because we did not have enough players (negative).

Reframe: Thanks to testing (positive) we called the game off to not put people at risk (positive).

The word "reframing" is very powerful and when used correctly can be very effective not if put into lies and back to the honesty part not everything needs to be negative.

Understand your situation and then deliver in the right way if a player is struggling with a skill say "killing the ball", they can't drop the heel and the ball keeps rolling under then tell them the where they are getting right and try or can you try and push your heal down even if you take them to one side and show them and let them do just the heel bit.

Chapter 4: The 15 Behaviours of EQ

Just to let you all know I am an **accredited EQ assessor** and have spent many years working with people and myself to understand why we have these emotions and how we can develop them to strengthen our relationships in work and sports.

What does EQ stand for? Well, it simply means Emotional Intelligence.

We are going to look at how we can use our emotional intelligence and the behaviours that make up our emotions. The diagram below shows the model for EQ.

EQ Stands for Emotional Quotient. Just like IQ measures your intelligence, your EQ is a measure of your emotions. Your ability to handle diversity and challenges with "emotional intelligence" is more responsible for your success than your IQ.

For example, when struck off in traffic, someone with a low EQ might scream, curse, and actually chase or tailgate the driver who caused the traffic, risking their safety over something that can give them no long-term gain. They are ruled by their emotions. Someone with a high EQ is in control of their emotions enough to realize that there's nothing they can do about the situation and the smart thing would be to continue on with their day.

Another example is when, someone with a low EQ might say "I'm depressed today, I'm not going to go to work" while someone with a high EQ might say "I'm depressed but staying home won't help me. I'll end up losing money and I won't feel any better moping around the house anyway".

Whilst it has been widely accepted that there was something beyond IQ and personality, EQ was first introduced as a concept by Reuven Bar-On in the 1980s and emotional intelligence was defined in the 1990s by Jack Mayer and Peter Salovey. Daniel Goleman popularised the term in his seminal work "Emotional Intelligence: Why it can matter more than IQ" in 1995 and it is becoming more and more accepted as a hugely significant factor in people's ability to succeed.

A broad definition of emotional intelligence is 'the ability to recognise, interpret and manage emotions – in yourself and others – to create better self-awareness and stronger, more meaningful relationships with others.'

Whilst genetics and upbringing have a clear impact on emotional intelligence, the great news for us all is that our levels can be improved and developed with coaching and practice.

The simplest way to enhance emotional intelligence is to understand the major factors that impact each skill and develop behaviours that enable people to cope better with all the emotions that they experience – internal and external.

These are the 5 composites as mentioned below.

Self-perception is made up of **self-regard, self-actualisation** and **emotional self-awareness**. It focuses on your "inner self" and determines how you are in touch with your feelings, how good you feel about yourself, and about what you're doing in life. It is about accepting yourself for who you are, not necessarily who you want to be.

Self-expression deals with **emotional expression, assertiveness,** and **independence**. It captures your ability to communicate your feelings constructively using both verbal and non-verbal skills and deals with your ability to make decisions without undue input or influence from others.

Interpersonal covers skills including **interpersonal relationships, empathy** and **social responsibility**. People with good levels of interpersonal skills tend to be responsible and dependable, and they create and develop sound relationships based on trust and reliability.

Decision Making focuses on **problem solving, reality testing** and **impulse control**. It measures an individual's ability to use their emotions positively to help them make the right decisions and the best choices. Good skills in the area will allow people to create solid solutions, based on reality and avoid disruptive impulses.

Stress Management incorporates **flexibility, stress tolerance** and **optimism**. The pace of change means that successful people are going to remain calm under pressure, accept that things are going to change (perhaps faster than they would like) and remain confident that they will still achieve the success they desire.

Now time to look at the 15 behaviours you see above in the 5 composites. Let's go through all 15, and learn their meanings, strengths, and weaknesses before we look at some examples on how we can improve these behaviours and where we will see them in our coaching.

You will see, as this chapter goes on, we use the words "low" and "high" and that a high score doesn't always mean good as it can cost for other behaviours. A more balanced approach over the 15 behaviours is recommended. When we look at the low scale of an assessment then we need to understand is there a cost of high impacting on the lows.

1. Self-Perception

Self-regard

This means respecting oneself while understanding and accepting one's strengths and weaknesses.

Often associated with feelings of inner strength and self-confidence.

LOW	HIGH
Unsure of self	Self-assured
Lack of self-esteem	Accepting of self
Low self-esteem	High self-esteem
Unhappy with physical appearance	Good sense of self
Not confident	Confident
	Fulfilled

Some follow up questions to ask your players if you see or hear your players show or talk these feelings:

1. What do you believe are your strengths? Provide an example where you used your strengths to your advantage.

2. Which of your abilities require development? Provide an example where you have had to work around/compensate for an area of weakness.

3. Describe a situation where you had to overcome feelings of insecurity or low confidence in your abilities.

4. Tell me about a time when it was clear you made a mistake or an error. How did you feel and what was your reaction?

Did you take to rectify the situation? Why do you think you felt this way?

5. How can you use your strengths to achieve more of your goals (personal or job performance)?

How can you overcome weaknesses on the way to achieving your goals?

6. What are you willing to do to improve your skills, abilities, habits, and attitudes?

Self-actualisation

This means the willingness to persistently try to improve oneself and engage in the pursuit of personally relevant and meaningful objectives that lead to a rich and enjoyable life.

LOW	HIGH
Life lacks meaning	A full, rich life
Unsure where to go in life	Activities have meaning
Not pursuing enjoyable things	Self-satisfied
Unmotivated	Energized
	Passionate and enthusiastic
	Motivated to do best

Some follow up questions to ask your players if you see or hear your players show or talk these feelings:

1. How do your emotions affect other people? Can you provide an example where your teamwork? (or a relationship) was affected by the way you were feeling?

2. What things do you feel really happy about? Sad? Angry? Describe how you experience these emotions physically, behaviourally, and cognitively.

3. Describe a time when you were making a decision and your emotions got the best of you?

What emotion were you experiencing and what was your reaction?

4. What emotions help your job performance? Which emotions hinder your performance?

5. Are there emotions that you are more comfortable with than others? Why do you think so?

Emotional self-awareness

This includes recognising and understanding one's own emotions.

It is the ability to differentiate between subtleties in one's own emotions while understanding the cause of these emotions and the impact they have on the thoughts and actions of oneself and others.

LOW	HIGH
Hard time verbalising own emotions	Rlates own feelings to appropriate causes
Difficulty recognizing, identifying own emotions	Understands changing of emotions
Low self-awareness	Self-aware
Avoids emotional ownership	In touch with own feelings
Surprised by others' reactions	Reads people well
Misreading and misread by people	People read you well

Some follow up questions to ask your players if you see or hear your players show or talk these feelings:

1. How do your emotions affect other people? Can you provide an example where your teamwork (or a relationship) was affected by the way you were feeling?

2. What things do you feel really happy about? Sad? Angry? Describe how you experience these emotions physically, behaviourally, and cognitively.

3. Describe a time when you were making a decision and your emotions got the best of you?

What emotion were you experiencing and what was your reaction?

4. What emotions help your job performance? Which emotions hinder your performance?

5. Are there emotions that you are more comfortable with than others? Why do you think so?

2. Self-expression

Emotional expression

Openly expression one's feelings verbally and non-verbally

LOW	HIGH
A closed book	Expresses self easily
An enigma	An open book
May appear withdrawn	Real

Some follow up questions to ask your players if you see or hear your players show or talk these feelings:

1. Are there some emotions you feel more comfortable expressing than others? Why do you think that is?

How do you express what you are feeling? Give examples.

2. Describe a time when you regretted not having expressed your true thoughts or feelings about something.

What were the consequences (positive and negative) of not expressing your feelings? How would the situation have been different had you been more expressive?

3. In general, do you find yourself bottling up emotions? How does this affect your ability to get your work done?

4. What does being happy look like to you? Being angry? Being frustrated?

5. Have others ever misread your feelings or thoughts? Why do you think that happened?

Assertiveness

This means communicating feelings, beliefs, and thoughts openly, and defending personal rights and values in a socially acceptable, non-offensive, and non-destructive manner.

LOW	HIGH
Passive	Express self easily
Shy	Defends rights in a non destructive manner
Overly controlled	Not overly controlled or shy
Unable to express self	Non-abusive but forthright
Quick to compromise	

Some follow up questions to ask your players if you see or hear your players show or talk these feelings:

1. Describe a scenario in which you behaved assertively. What specifically did you do or say that was assertive?

2. What do you find challenging about being assertive? What is it about the context or situation that makes you uncomfortable standing up for yourself?

3. How would you react if someone on your team consistently failed to pull their weight on a team project?

4. What is the difference between assertive and aggressive behaviour? Have you ever been perceived as being aggressive?

How do you know?

5. Tell me about a time when you disagreed with someone. What did you do/say and what was the outcome?

Independence

It is the ability to be self-directed and free from emotional dependency on others.

Decision-making, planning, and daily tasks are completed autonomously.

LOW	HIGH
Needs protection or support	Self-directed
Uncertain of own ideas	self-determined
Indecisive	Decisive
Lets others make final decisions	Free from emotional dependence
Lacks confidence	Confident

Some follow up questions to ask your players if you see or hear your players show or talk these feelings:

1. Describe your typical style for making decisions.

2. Can you give an example of when you relied on others to make a decision for you? What was the outcome?

3. What feelings do you experience when you need to work independently from others?

Do these feelings change (i.e., become more or less intense) over time?

4. To what extent do you involve others in the decisions you make?

5. Can you describe a situation where you went against the grain and made a decision that was not the popular choice?

What was the outcome?

3. Interpersonal

Interpersonal relationships

It is the ability to develop and maintain mutually satisfying relationships that are characterised by trust and compassion.

LOW	HIGH
Does not like intimacy	Ability to establish mutually satisfying relationships
Not giving	Ability to give and take affection and imtimacy
Not interested in relationships	Maintains relationships over time
Not able to share feelings	Looks positively at social change
Loner	Feels at ease in social situations

Some follow up questions to ask your players if you see or hear your players show or talk these feelings:

1. Describe a time when you had to mediate a conflict between team members. Describe a time when you had to deal with an

interpersonal conflict with a team member. How did your emotions differ between experiences?

2. What efforts do you put in to maintaining healthy and effective relationships at work?

How do you know when a working relationship is effective?

3. Describe what types of social situations make you feel uncomfortable. What is your typical response in these situations?

4. Tell me about a time when you had to put extra effort into maintaining a close relationship.

What value did this relationship have in your life?

5. Has there ever been a time when your relationships have made it difficult to make a decision or get your work done?

Empathy

It includes recognizing, understanding, and appreciating how other people feel.

Involves being able to articulate your understanding of another's perspective and behaving in a way that respects others' feelings.

LOW	HIGH
Can't understand people's feelings	Sensitive to feelings of others
Has difficulties relating to others	Able to put self in "others' shoes"
Surprised by others' reaction	Anticipates others' reactions
Misreads social cues	Picks up on social cues

Some follow up questions to ask your players if you see or hear your players show or talk these feelings:

1. Tell me about a time when it was really important that you were able to understand the way someone else felt.

How did you convey this understanding? How did you ensure you understood them?

2. Describe a situation where you were not as sensitive to someone's feelings as you should have been.

Why do you think this was the case? What could you have done differently?

3. In your opinion, what is the difference between sympathy and empathy? How do you ensure you display these differently?

4. How do you ensure you have really understood how another person is feeling?

5. Describe a situation where you found it difficult to make a decision because of the way the outcome might impact others.

What was the result of your decision?

Social responsibility

It includes willingly contributing to society, to one's social groups, and generally to the welfare of others.

It involves acting responsibly, having social consciousness, and showing concern for the greater community.

LOW	HIGH
Unwilling to be involved in group or team	Cooperative
Hesitant to commit to group activities	Gives and contributes to group
Difficulty following through on group tasks	Responsible and dependable
	Feels genuine concern for others in the group

Some follow up questions to ask your players if you see or hear your players show or talk these feelings:

1. What have you done recently to help those in need?

2. Describe a situation where you have placed others' needs/interests over your own.

How often does this type of scenario occur in your life?

3. How do you define "being a team player" in your job? What are some examples of where your success can be attributed to your team and not to you alone?

4. What social issues are of particular concern to you? How do you contribute to these causes?

5. Provide an example of when you had to take responsibility for your actions. How did this make you feel?

4. Decision Making

Problem solving

It is the ability to find solutions to problems in situations where emotions are involved.

Includes the ability to understand how emotions impact decision making.

LOW	HIGH
Jumps into solution	Gathers information first, weighs pros and cons
Flies by seat of pants	Can identify and solve problems
Uses unstructured strategy	Uses a systematic approach

Some follow up questions to ask your players if you see or hear your players show or talk these feelings:

1. What was one of the most challenging problems you have ever had to solve?

Describe the problem-solving process you used to arrive at the solution.

2. How do you think your problem-solving process looks to those you work with?

What would they say are strengths of this process? What would they say you could do better?

3. Describe a time when your emotions hampered your ability to make a decision. Why did you get sidetracked?

4. What role do your emotions play in your problem-solving process? How do they help or hinder your ability to arrive at a solution?

5. Tell me about a time when you made a rash decision. What caused this to happen and how did it affect others?

Reality testing

It is the capacity to remain objective by seeing things as they really are.

It involves recognizing when emotions or personal bias can cause one to be less objective.

LOW	HIGH
Tuned out	Tuned into environment
Unrealistic	Can assess life situations fairly accurately
Disconnected	Grounded

Some follow up questions to ask your players if you see or hear your players show or talk these feelings:

1. Would you describe yourself as a realist or an idealist? How does this description manifest itself in your job?

2. Describe a time where you incorrectly sized up a situation. What information did you misjudge and what was the impact?

3. How would others describe the goals you set? What information do you take into account when you set these goals?

4. Tell me about a time when you should have been more objective rather than relying on a "gut feeling".

How do you confirm that your "gut feeling" is accurate?

5. Tell me about a time when you should have listened to your instincts rather than being so objective. How do you confirm that your instincts are reliable?

Impulse control

It is the ability to resist or delay an impulse, drive, or temptation to act.

It involves avoiding rash behaviours and decision making.

LOW	HIGH
Explosive and unpredictable	Composed
Lack of anger control	Good control of aggression
Abusive	Ability to delay or resist an impulse
Easily frustrated	High tolerance to frustration
Aggressive	Patient

Some follow up questions to ask your players if you see or hear your players show or talk about these feelings:

1. How do you typically deal with an impulse to act?

2. Tell me about a time when you had to exercise patience and control over your behaviour.

3. Describe a situation where you were impatient and reacted hastily. How did this impact the end result?

4. Describe a situation where it was beneficial for you to act quickly. How did this make you feel?

5. Has your impulsiveness ever created problems for you? How do you think others view your behaviour in these instances?

5. Stress Management

Flexibility

It means adapting emotions, thoughts, and behaviours to unfamiliar, unpredictable, and dynamic circumstances or ideas.

LOW	HIGH
Rigid	Able to adapt to changing conditions
Hard to change	Open to new views, change of behaviour
Stuck in patterns	Going with the flow
Status quo	

Some follow up questions to ask your players if you see or hear your players show or talk about these feelings:

1. Would others say that you are flexible and open to change, or rigid and set in your ways?

What benefits and drawbacks does your typical style bring to your workplace?

2. How do you successfully manage change in an environment where people are hesitant to depart with their old ways of doing things?

3. Give an example of where you found it difficult to adjust to a change in your job. What emotions were you feeling?

4. Do you prefer your work to be predictable and stable, or do you enjoy conditions that require you to change what you do?

5. Describe a time where you have to adjust quickly to changes in your environment.

What was your process for changing your behaviour/tasks?

Stress tolerance

It is all about coping with stressful or difficult situations and believing that one can manage or influence situations in a positive manner.

LOW	HIGH
Lacking or ineffective coping mechanisms	Effective coping mechanisms
Reactive	Calm and maintaining control
Fearful	Optimistic towards change
High anxiety levels	Stable and relaxed

Some follow up questions to ask your players if you see or hear your players show or talk about these feelings:

1. How do you tackle stressful circumstances at work? What is an example of where you had to manage stress in order to get your job done?

2. What circumstances are stressful for you? How do you proactively manage these circumstances in order to reduce the stress, you experience?

3. How does stress manifest itself in the way you feel (i.e., emotionally, physically) or act?

Can you detect the very onset of stress in your body?

4. What strategies do you use to cope with stress? How much do these strategies rely on support from others?

5. Describe a time when it was important for you to remain calm under pressure.

What skills or techniques did you use? How were others impacted in this situation?

Optimism

It is an indicator of one's positive attitude and outlook on life.

It involves remaining hopeful and resilient, despite occasional setbacks.

LOW	HIGH
Fear worst will happen	Positive attitude in face of adversity
Pessimistic	Hopeful approach to life
Uncertain about the future	Confident about the future

Some follow up questions to ask your players if you see or hear your players show or talk about these feelings:

1. Would you describe yourself as having positive or negative expectations about how things will turn out?

How does this impact the way you set goals and objectives?

2. Describe a project/task where you experienced several setbacks. What was your approach to overcoming these difficulties?

3. When planning and setting goals, how do you manage risk? What does your contingency plan look like?

4. Describe a situation where you were overly positive or overly negative in your expectations about how things would turn out.

What impact did your outlook have on your performance and that of others?

5. What are some resources or strategies you draw upon in order to stay positive about the future?

Now that you know the 15 behaviours and what they mean in "low" and "high" points, we can go through a few scenarios and then maybe think about your players and certain signs they show. You can look at how you can help to strengthen the low points and also if any cost of high points.

An example of cost of high in self-regards would be what I call it the "X factor" syndrome. People come to the show and think they can sing but the judges and people who watch them cry with laughter not because they can't sing but because they still believe they can. (believe not think they are better than they really are).

We will not cover the assessment side in this book, but I will give a little background on it.

Most people need to understand themselves first and then others. We call this self-awareness (what do I think) and social awareness (what do they think).

The assessment has 133 questions. No right or wrong answers. It is just what you honestly think. It takes 20 to 25 minutes to complete and once you get the report, you are scored on the 15 behaviours. We can look at results and balance of score to find the areas that we need to develop.

For more info on this assessment, drop me an e-mail at:

jasonpyott@gmail.com

This is how the assessment report looks:

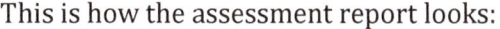

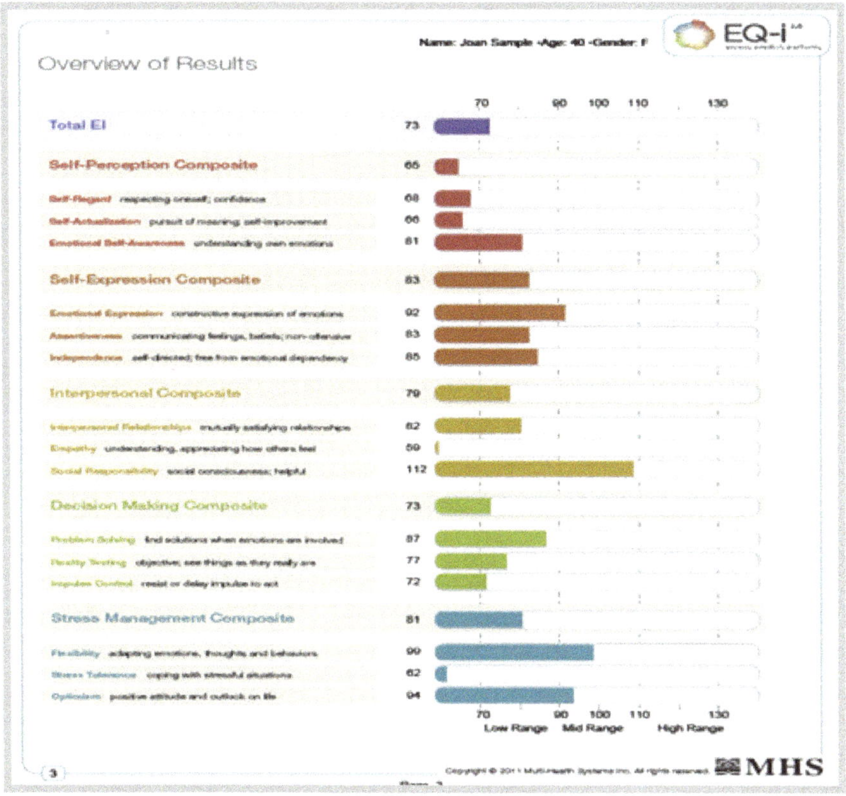

Using your scores to look at development.

Scenario 1: Little Tommy turns up to training every week and runs up to the coach to say "hello". At the start of the session, Tommy asks questions for more information and then goes off to practice that information giving his best. But as the coach makes the drill more challenging and steps up the pace, Tommy starts to struggle and he gets frustrated to the point he stops trying and it starts to impact the drill and his group. Tommy sits out and cries, while breathing fast as he is very upset.

So, now we need first to understand the behaviours in which Tommy is high and the behaviours in which Tommy is low.

Let's break down the scenario. Tommy seems happy so has a full rich life, energized, passionate and enthusiastic, open book. I could go even deeper on this one little scenario, but this will be enough to get you thinking about your players and the scenarios you have experienced. I would say, on the high side, the two behaviours that Tommy shows in this scenario are **emotional expression** and **self-actualisation**

Now, let's take a look at the part of the scenario when Tommy started to struggle and lose confidence and focus. The coach decided to make the drill more challenging because he thought it was too slow or the lads were finding it too easy (all the lads?) or is it because the coach had to get through the session and needed to move on even if the players were not ready. I hear you saying, "Well, we were not there so how would we know?" But with just a scenario I can tell that Tommy was not ready as he was so positive at the start and went off to put the information into practice. Remember how happily he says "hello" and asks questions but by the end struggles with the drill, which becomes more challenging. He shows anxiety with his breathing and crying, and also he becomes fearful of the drill and the impact on the group to the level that he feels he should sit out. Also, Tommy has not thought about the impact on the other players and how that makes them feel, his low self-awareness avoiding his low self-awareness. What two behaviours do you think Tommy needs some development? I would say, on the low side, the two behaviours that Tommy shows are **stress tolerance** and **emotional self-awareness**.

Let's now look at scenario 2

The coach tells Tommy to get up, stop crying, and join the group; Tommy gets up still crying and goes back to the group. But he still struggles and tries his best till the end of the session. At the end, the coach calls the players in and makes a point on saying "make sure when you come for training you bring the right attitude" and then the players leave.

Let's look at the coaching point of view and ask ourselves what emotion did the coach lack by telling Tommy to get back into the group? Yes, you got it right – **Empathy** (try walking a mile in that person's shoes before saying anything). The coach could have sat with Tommy and asked why he was so upset, calm him down, and slowly make him join back to the session. This would not only have less impact on the other players but also keep the standard of the drill high.

I know it is very hard to keep all players happy but this is where having not only a technical knowledge but also an EQ knowledge will make the sessions a much happier environment for all the players, stop and think. Remember one of the best development methods for EQ is the easiest **count to ten**. We will look at the brain and how it works in a later chapter.

You think about all the coaches and managers from grassroots, the professional game, and the ones that you think are great. You will find that they possess a high EQ and learn how to work with people from all backgrounds and types (four types of people).

Know yourself as well as your self-awareness, and know your players as well as your social awareness.

All you can do is understand where you are today, and look at ways to improve and develop.

The last section of the 15 behaviours is about well-being. Why is this not part of the 15 behaviours? Well, I will explain.

Happiness

Happiness is an indicator of the emotional health and well-being, rather than a subscale of any area in particular, characterized by feeling of satisfaction, contentment, and the ability to enjoy the many aspects of one's life.

It does not directly contribute to your total EQ-i2.0 score

The four behaviours most often associated with happiness are self-regard, interpersonal relationships, optimism, and self-actualisation.

It is very important that we are happy in what we do.

Chapter 5: 4 Ts of Change

Change... well, this is a very interesting subject because if I had one pound for every time I heard someone say "people don't like change", I would be a rich man.

Before we go into this subject, I will make it clear it's not the change that people don't like and, in this chapter, I will explain why and how if we use the 4 Ts change is accepted and even welcomed.

So, I hear you asking, "What these 4 Ts are?" We will go through a scenario where you will be taking a plane trip. All you need to do is read it carefully and write down your decisions. Let's prepare ourselves for the take-off.

You will have a few questions to answer. None of them are tricky questions, so take your time and answer them honestly.

You are flying on your own for a game to meet up with your team as the head coach, leaving from your local airport. The plane has three types of tickets: first class, middle class, and cattle class. You are sitting in the middle-class seats.

Once you are seated, the flight attendant comes up to you and offers you a seat in first class. (No tricky questions, remember?) What is your decision?

Ok, most of us would accept the upgrade and enjoy the flight, because it was something we know is better than middle class, the decision is made easy.

Now the fun starts. What would you do if the flight attendant comes up to you and says, "sir/madam could you move back to cattle class?" What's your answer?

Now, those with low impulse control (one of the 15 behaviours) might say straight away NO, and those with high impulse control might ask the question "why", get the facts, and then maybe still say "no".

Imagine if the flight attendant comes up and says, "The lady next to you has her disabled son sitting in the cattle class as she could not get the second ticket in middle class. Would it be ok with you if you swop places with her son before take-off as he needs monitoring and looking after? Now what is your answer?

Yes, most of the people after learning this information would move, but why? We have not gone up in the planes comfort but down and yes, I know people will say that it's about the situation with the boy but when they were just asked to move without telling the reason, the answer was "no". So, we hit the first **T** for **transparency**. Without spoiling the other three, I will list them now.

Transparency

Trust

Truth

Time

So, now let's look at what the flight attendant said on which the 4 Ts came into play and allowed you to make this decision. **Transparency** - well this is the whole story of why they asked you to move. On the **trust** side, we all trust the flight attendants as we see them as people of authority and knowledge when it comes to flying. A little bit at times like a strict teacher or smiling assassin or looking at the trust formula they are very creditable (know the job), reliable (always there), and have plenty of intimacy (share knowledge) with most of the focus on the people on the flight, so their self-focus in at a good level.

You were given **time** by the flight attendant as you were asked if you could move before they take-off and from the beginning the whole **truth** was put to you. So you could make your decision with all the 4 Ts in place and I would say 99% of people would move.

Let's look at the above scenario with each of the 4 Ts missing.

Transparency

Flight attendant says "would you move to cattle class NOW"

Well, we have the time in the word "NOW". You have no reason not to trust the flight attendant and no reason to doubt the truth as not much has been said. But without the transparency of why you need to move, how does it make you feel? Depending on how you are as a person will help quickly make up your decision.

Trust

Flight attendant says "Hello, I'm on my second flight ever and on my first one I didn't know much about flying and safety. Oh, I need to ask if you could move to the cattle class before the flight takes off as we have a very sick boy who he needs to sit next to his mother. She in the seat next to you, but they could not get a ticket together. Would this be ok with you?"

So, how do you feel when you hear that they were on their second flight and didn't do very well on the first one? Yes, I agree that we cannot trust much this fight attendant but they still gave you time by asking if you can move before the flight takes off. Transparency of why they want you to move is seen and they told you the truth.

Truth

Flight attendant says, "Hello, can we ask you to move to cattle class before we take off as your seat needs to be kept free to keep the plane balanced? The only person who can sit on this seat is a child and we have one in cattle class. Can we swap his place with you? Now we know the time is in place again with the "before we take off" and the flight attendant showed transparency. You trust them as they are the experts, but you know deep down that the reason for moving felt like a lie and now you start to wonder about how much trust you feel for them and was it as transparent as it could have been.

Time

Flight attendant says, "Hello would it be ok with you if we ask you to move to the cattle class for the take-off? It will only be until the seat belt lights go off. We have a very sick, little boy who needs to sit next to his mum in the seat to your right".

The flight takes off and the fasten seat belt lights go off and 30 minutes later you are still sitting in the cattle class seat.

Now it is very transparent and no reason not to trust them as they are the professionals and why would they not tell the truth about the sick boy. But weather they forgot or thought you would be ok, the time side has gone and you feel to let down which starts to make you feel you weren't told the truth and now you have lost trust in them as well.

So, if any of the 4 Ts are missing when trying to implement change, it will cause problems and people will revert to say comments like "people don't like change".

Now we have a deeper understanding of the 4 Ts of change we can look at our coaching and see if we can put them into play in a typical session.

Well let's take a session. Normally we train on a Tuesday night between 6 to 7 pm but this week we need to train on Thursday night between 7 to 8 pm.

If we look at this change as the players and parents, we will not only see this is a different day but also 1 hour later.

Text one to parents and players is: "Hi, we will be training on Thursday between 7 to 8 pm this week. Thanks, Carl.

Now, trust me when I say if your phone would be off the hook with people ringing with different issues and concerns, as it does not suit them day wise and time wise, just take a minute to think how we could change this text to be more transparent, truthful, time, reason, trustful.

Text two to parents and players: Hello, hope you are all well. Would it be ok if we looked at training on Thursday night between 7 to 8 pm? I know this is a different day and time but I have been asked to work until 6.30 pm on Tuesday and will not make it to Tuesday's training on time. I need to be there as the session needs two coaches. I know this could cause issues and if you need support getting your lads to training please drop me a line and we will support any way we can. I hope you understand and look forward to seeing you for this one week on Thursday. All the best, Carl.

Now this is very transparent and you have told the parents and players the truth with a time scale of one week.. As the coach they have a trust in you as you are creditable and reliable, and sharing the information whilst not making it all about you wanting to help the boys get to training, right level of self-focus.

One last scenario is around a player having to change position and a true story.

I was and still am the coach of then under 13s team and had attracted two new strikers who were very technically good and very fast. Also I had two other strikers technically very good but one of them was lacking the speed of the other three. When we counter attacked, he was left behind and struggled to join the attack back and his fitness was not at the level needed. This went on for about half a season and I could see the lad struggling and unhappy with his football. This lad was on the smaller pitches, a very good striker who finished and kicked the ball well, but as the pitches got bigger, the gap started to form. I wish I realized this earlier, but we all learn from our mistakes and where he was playing most of the game, he started only managing half or just a bit more every game. I didn't realise the impact it was having on him and his Dad as he was getting frustrated with the lad and me or should I say me and his lad until one game. He exploded at me and told me what he thought about his son not playing as much time as he had used to.

So, I kept calm and went home quite upset. Yes, we coaches do have feelings and it reflected on what had just happened. I did see it but never did anything to improve the situation. The next training session I sat with the lad and not his Dad and asked him to tell me how he feels about his football, where it is going. He was open enough to let me know he was struggling with the pace of the game up front and didn't know what to do. Then I asked him if I could suggest something to him about looking to change his position which I know was hard for the lad but he knew if he wanted to play at this level with his mates, something had to change. So, I suggested him to play centre back as he will have less running to do. He was the biggest lad in the team and could kick a ball very well and was one of the best at heading the ball.

When his Dad came to pick him up, we had a conversation and I told him my plans. By now, the Dad had calmed down and we both said sorry for what happened in the game. I told him though he's not my son, I do love all these lads.

This was one of the best pieces of coaching I have down in my eyes as we got the lad back loving the game and we as a team got a very strong defender and he also won "the player of the season". The time you think you have missed the boat but it is better late than ever. The one thing you don't want to do is know the boat is there but not go at all.

Remember, change is not the issue but how we handle that change should always be transparent, truthful, time, factual, trustworthy and the change you want/need to make can go smoothly.

Just think not all changes are good but can still be done and understood by those being asked to change.

Example:

New footballs for the team. The lads like the ones they use but they have got a bit worn and out of shape, but even if better balls but how would you explain this to the players.

"Lads, we've got some new balls. These are the latest designs and the best quality in the market, used by "such and such" clubs". This will be a very easy change for the players.

"Lads got some new balls, not as good as the last ones as we don't have the budget for better ones. We all know the old ones are worn and out of shape" again changing for less but explained in the right way that the players understand why and accept it.

Chapter 6: Blue Chair, Pink Chair

This chapter is all about when we think we know what we want, but do we really?

I designed an experiment to show people that they think they know what training and development they need, but this experiment shows the "do they".

We have all seen the one type of education, training, development fits all taking off the self-leadership courses. Yes, we can all learn from this but are we all getting the most for our needs and how do we truly know what our needs are if we don't understand where we are in our self-awareness and social awareness?

So when look at coaching, yes, we have some very good courses from the FA on all sorts of subjects but the spine of the path is level 1, level 2, UEFA B, UEFA A, and pro license, and in these courses they have information on styles and feelings. It's nice to work on the emotions that you are high on but we also need to work on those in which we have a low score as well. Where in these courses help you with, say, stress tolerance or impulse control well, they are in them in small bits if you know what to look for but not steering you in the face.

I have worked with a lot of H.R (human resource) people in my years as a senior manager and it amazes me to this day to think about how many really don't get the needs of their people (not all H.R, covers me). It's like any course you take and get the piece of paper to say

I'm now qualified to do this and this but until you put those skills to practice and challenge what you have learnt, does it make me the person the paper says I am.

Example: true story

I will use the one from work, but you can turn the same thought pattern into football coaching.

In our management team we had seven people reporting to me – OPS director, Finance Director, H.R Director, Maintenance Manager, Engineering manager, Logistics Manager, and Sales Director.

Every week, we had a management meeting for around 1 to 2 hours and each senior manager had a presentation. They went through the KPI's (key performance indicators). At the end of the meeting, I use to do my presentation and people didn't realise how important it is for me to go last as too many people follow the HIPPO approach in management. What is HIPPO approach? Well, let me tell you.

Highest

Paid

Person's

Opinion

You will find that if the highest paid (or highest position in coaching) starts the meeting on his presentation and views, then there is a high chance that the rest will follow his views. Any good leader (coach) will know it is good to get different opinions and views and for those people who just sit back and agree, you will never get the best from them.

One day my Maintenance Manager was on a holiday and he chose the Maintenance Supervisor to take his place in the management meeting. He was a good man and lots of knowledge of the company.

To put it in blunt turns (German 4 types of people) he had a nightmare when presenting the facts and figures, his excel numbers were all over the place. The next day I asked him to come and have a coffee with me as I knew he was hurting from his performance. He felt he had let himself and me down.

I explained that we need to understand what he thought went wrong and how we can work on improving this area. He was up for it and said he felt better for the chat. So he went off with a meeting booked in place with me for the next day. The next day arrived. We sat down and I asked him what did he think was the area he needed some development in. He said that he sat with the H.R Director and they think it was the excel training that was required to which I said ok let's take a look at that.

Ok, let's talk about the excel side. Can I ask you if any figures you presented were incorrect, and he replied "no". Did the excel calculations not add up and he replied "no". So my next question was, "why you think it was excel?" He had no real reply so I asked, "How did you feel in the meeting?" He said in his words (not mine) "I was shitting myself" to which I laughed and then asked, "Why were you nervous?" He replied, "I was delivering in the management group for the first time, which made me panic. I had a very dry mouth and lots my focus with worry."

"Great", I said to him and he replied, "What do you mean great?" Well now we are getting deeper into this. We can rule out the excel and look at your emotions, I have a question for you – "how many times do you have a meeting with your reports?" He replied every day that means five times a week. "How does it go normally for you?" He replied, "very well and very structured." But how do you feel in this meeting. He said, "I feel confident." Ok, is that because the information and excel is correct? He replied, "No, because I know the people well and the environment we are in." And then I said, "Jackpot!"

I told him that I have failed in the meeting yesterday to which he asked, "How is that so?" I explained him that I should have given you some time during the week with all the senior managers on a personal side, where you get to meet and understand them in a deeper manner, so to make you feel at ease in the meeting. Not just see the badges but also see them as people. Also I saw that you were panicking and could have offered you some water, or even better, could have spent some time at the beginning of the meeting having a chat about a subject you like and feel comfortable around.

So, you see the employee thought his excel let him down but realized it were his emotions that were running wild. We then put him on an EQ development course and to this day I still speak to him.

So, it is not always what we think is correct for us. Now I'm going to explain why this chapter is called the pink chair and the white chair.

Pink chair and white chair experiment

I have done this experiment at a few talks that did on "culture" and "what development do I need" events.

Let me paint the picture for you. You have arrived at an event in a hall full of 250 people.

On the stage, there is a blue chair and a pink chair. I'm standing on the left-hand side of the stage and have the pink chair next to me and the blue chair next to the pink chair, which is on the right-hand side.

I start talking to the audience about training for them and their teams. Then I say to them that I will be asking one man (pointing with arm to blue chair) and one woman (pointing to pink chair) to come up on stage, but not to worry we will not be asking you to do anything.

I start by choosing a man from the crowd (any man) and as he walks up on to the stage, I ask him to take a seat pointing to the blue chair. Let me also say, for your information, the blue chair is nearest to the steps on to the stage.

Guess which chair the man sits on? Yes, you got it right. The blue chair.

Now, I do not ask for the lady as they don't realise the experiment is complete, and this is what happens next.

I ask all the audience to check under their seats and pick up the three cards lying on the floor.

Each card has a different word:

Card 1 says: Style

Card 2 says: Colour

Card 3 says: Comfort

I now ask the audience one simple question, "If given only one chair to sit on for the rest of your life, what will you look for – style, colour, or comfort?"

Go on, answer it and we all know the answer would be COMFORT.

So, why did the man (all do it) go to the blue chair? Well, there are some good reasons, but one strong reason was, we know that blue is associated with men. Also I pointed to blue chair when talking about getting a man up and the blue chair was set nearest to steps to the stage and again, I lead him with my arm.

Now, we know the colour would probably be for men number three out of three and two for the ladies. But when we are giving the right question from the start we will get better ideas of true development that we need to progress in our coaching. Ask others their views, ask people in the same game, ask people in the right profession. We will have lots of options to get it right, but remember one of the 15 behaviours being impulse control and sometimes we do have time to look at the facts before jumping in.

If the first question I asked you in the hall was – "What out of these three factors do you think matters most when buying a chair"?

Style

Colour

Comfort

"Ok Sir, can you come on stage and sit in the chair that fits your choice"? Then we all know that he would go and sit on the pink chair.

We think we know what we want but do we really?

Let's look at this in the football terms and think about the scenario as a coach.

Little Jonny is playing for your team and during the game you notice that little Jonny will not head the ball and keeps on letting it bounce. This puts the team under pressure. Half time arrives, and you tell little Jonny to head the ball and not let it bounce in a commanding style and he nods in agreement. But again through the second half, Jonny let's another 5 balls bounce that he should have off headed. After the game you tell Jonny he will be doing heading practice at training and Jonny says, "Great, as I need it."

Training arrives. You keep your word and have put up a heading session to have a big focus on how Jonny does as he is the only player in matches that does not head the ball.

You set up your drill. In pairs, the players throw the ball to each other. They try and head the ball back to the player who has throwing it. Jonny has no issues with this. It leaves you a little confused with why he does it so well in training and not in the game.

I see this a lot around so many different subjects in the game. As coaches, we are taught about making it game-realistic and getting a player to throw the ball from 5 meters away just isn't. Now if you are doing that for teaching the right technique then great and after a while you will see the players who get it and those who don't whether it be they don't watch the ball or didn't understand to use their forehead.

My advice is always to spend time with the players and try to understand why they struggle with such issues and see if they can give you the reason.

So, you ask Jonny to arrive 15 minutes before the training. You sit with him and ask why does he think, in the games he cannot head the ball. Jonny replies that he thinks if he heads it and gets it wrong it could hurt him and also that he might head it the wrong way and put the team under pressure. You then say, "But in training you do very well when we do heading drill." Jonny replies, "Yes, but the ball isn't coming from very high, so I know it will not hurt me." Old saying is what we know we can do.

Fantastic work, coach! Now we know how Jonny is thinking and we can see the different reasons for not heading the ball. Also, we can look at how we built the emotional state for how Jonny feels happy to header the ball as well as the physical needs of Jonny.

For me as a coach, I would agree with Jonny on how the session will look for him. Also at the end of the training make a contract with him that after the session we would look to see if you can head two balls in the game and any more would be a bonus. So, we know this is fear as an emotion for Jonny. One, it might hurt and two, not sure where the ball would go if Jonny does head it.

Let's look at the first part and the session that you might put on with the technique for how to head the ball and where we head the ball. Start with the players throwing for each other five meters away taking turns to head the ball. The next step might be a game on the goal cross bar almost like head tennis where the ball is coming from a higher height but with the players wanting to win the score points. The focus will be on heading the ball back over the cross bar but see what has been done by using a cross bar as net. The ball will be coming from a height of 7 to 8 feet or even higher. When Jonny has headed one ball, tell him what a good job that was and you might feel that's enough for one session for Jonny. If you feel that he has more to give and looks happy then put together something like a 10 x 10 meter square. Put four of them 10 meters apart each square. Divide the players into the four squares equally and get them to kick the ball high up and the square in which the ball is going to land, the players in that square cannot let the ball bounce as they will lose a point. The only way they can stop it is by heading the ball.

Watch Jonny's performance and see if he has headed this. Make sure at the end of session, you have five minutes to tell him what you have seen. Also make him go through session and get him to see what he has done. This will give him the confidence to get over his fear. It might take more than a session of course but don't forget the agreement you both made for the game. You can talk to Jonny about it before the game and tell him how well he did at training to give him that added confidence.

Again, we think we know what we need but do we really?

When we take that time to truly understand the needs behind the issue and don't just jump to first conclusion (impulse control), we make better decisions.

One of the best and oldest sayings around is "count to ten before you make a decision".

In a later chapter, we will be talking more about this and get a deeper understanding on how the brain works.

Chapter 7: 10 Reasons Why Top Talent Will Leave

1. **You failed to unleash their passions**: Smart companies align employee passions with corporate pursuits. Human nature makes it very difficult to walk away from areas of passion. If you fail to understand this, you'll unknowingly be encouraging employees to seek their passion elsewhere.

2. **You failed to challenge their intellect:** Smart people don't like to live in a dimly lit world of boredom. If you don't challenge people's minds, they'll leave you for someone/someplace that will.

3. **You failed to engage their creativity:** Great talent is wired to improve, enhance, and add value. They are built to change and innovate. They NEED to contribute by putting their fingerprints on design. Smart leaders don't place people in boxes – they free them from boxes. What's the use in having a racehorse if you don't let them run?

4. **You failed to develop their skills**: Leadership isn't a destination – it's a continuum. No matter how smart or talented a person is, there's always room for growth, development, and continued maturation. If you place restrictions on a person's ability to grow, they'll leave you for someone who won't.

5. **You failed to give them a voice**: Talented people have good thoughts, ideas, insight, and observations. If you don't listen to them, I can guarantee you someone will.

6. **You failed to care**: Sure, people come to work for a pay check, but that's not the only reason. In fact, many studies show it's not even the most important reason. If you fail to care about people at a human level and an emotional level, they'll eventually leave you regardless of how much you pay them.

7. **You failed to Lead**: Businesses don't fail, products don't fail, projects don't fail, and teams don't fail – leaders fail. The best testament to the value of coaching is what happens in its absence –very little. If you fail to lead, your talent will seek leadership elsewhere.

8. **You failed to recognise their contributions**: The best coaches don't take credit; they give it. Failing to recognize the contributions of others, is not only arrogant and disingenuous, but it's also just as good as asking them to leave.

9. **You failed to increase their responsibility**: You cannot confine talent; try to do so and you'll either devolve into mediocrity, or force your talent seek more fertile ground. People will gladly accept a huge workload as long as an increase in responsibility comes along with the performance and execution of the said workload.

10. **You failed to keep your commitments**: Promises made are worthless but promises kept are invaluable. If you break trust of those who lead you will pay a very steep price. Coaches are not accountable to their people, but will eventually be held accountable by their people.

If Coaches spent less time trying to retain people, and more time trying to understand them, care for them, invest in them, and lead them well, the retention thing would take care of itself.

As a coach we look hard at the technical side and on how we want the players to learn and perform, but we need to spend as much time around the emotional side and different types of players from the emotional side as much as the technical side.

Chapter 8: Diversity in Full

Diversity is one of the most used words in business and sports at the moment, but do we really understand the meaning and how you can split the word "diversity" into two types?

Demographic diversity

Cognitive diversity

Let's talk about the first one and most commonly used one of the two, demographic diversity.

This is where we have a difference in race, gender, and class. If I was asking you to write down three words that mean diversity to you would these three above cover it?

Now let's talk about the second part of diversity, cognitive diversity.

This is where we have a difference in thoughts, insights, and prospections.

Now let's look at this scenario below:

A coach takes a local football team and all the boys and girls go to the same school. They are all of different races and religions, and are all of the same age (school year). They all play for the school team, which the club coach also takes as he is the P.E teacher of that school. All of the players live in the local area, which I would say is a middle class for this scenario.

So, if we look at the word diversity then most people would say this is a very diverse group of children and at first glance, I would agree. But when we split up the word diversity and now look at it from a cognitive perspective, it might start looking different.

These players have had only one coach for school and club and they will be taught one way the coaches' beliefs on coaching and trust me this can be so different between coaches.

Quick thought:

Parents ask, "Should I get my son to join your club?" I love my club. For me, the facilities are important but what is most important is the coaches' and club's philosophy on the game, and how it should be played and carried out. My advice would be to sit with the coaches in a local area and understand them as a person and if they have the technical ability qualification to coach your child.

You will also find that, the thought process between these players will be very similar and also the insight they have had. I want to be clear that the team has a lot of good going, different race groups, religion groups, and mixed gender. Never forget the dedication the P.E teacher has to not only coach this team at school but also coach them out of school.

This also works for coaches. Just think now you probably have an assistant coach for your team, someone you know very well and have the same views on the game. There is nothing wrong with it but just think if your assistant left and you were looking for a new assistant coach, again most people will go for what they know because for what we don't know, we usually think of it as negative.

In the professional game, you see a lot of coaches and there are a couple of good points to this as you can break training sessions down into more specific trainings or even position or unit (defence, midfield, attack). But another reason is they all bring fresh eyes on training and match day, and can give their own views, thoughts, and insight to how training and the game went. The physio might bring different views on the ground you train play on. It also could have thoughts on shape and fitness levels even though the club has a fitness coach and manager and coaching staff look at shape. Trust me, be open minded enough to take on views from people from different backgrounds as if you might get someone exactly the same as you, who will always agree, but cannot always get the problem solved.

We are going to look at a few different problems in a football club and see how they solve these issues.

Scenario 1:

You are coaching a team and you see one of your players is having problems in the way he moves. His style looks different and he lacks pace when he needs to accelerate. The first thing you do is ask your assistant coach what he sees, and he agrees that the way the player is running does slow him down when he needs to add pace and at times the game can leave him behind.

Both coaches agree to work with him at training on trying to get him to run quicker and put in place sprint training now this is where we think we are sorting the problem out. Great, we are showing individual development for the player but is it what the issue we are trying to get him to run quicker with the same method or do we need to look at the motion of his running?

Now when we look at the bigger picture or the whole issue, we need to think about what it is that is stopping the player from moving quickly at times during the game. Yes, as coaches you have identified this in a game but think who else might help to solve this problem. Would the physio be worth adding to the group to see it from maybe not a football technical stand point but from the movement of a player and body stress movement? Also could you ask parents if you could get a local running coach to come and have a look? Now we would have a wide range of diversity from different backgrounds which will give us more information to help with making the best decisions to improve the players' running motion and confidence.

So, what do I mean about wide range of diversity? Put simple, once we identify a problem then we need to solve it. This is where you probably have heard about "problem solving"? Now we will look at a few charts to show this in a visual format and understand how we can cover the problem from all different angles by having more diversity.

If we look at the grey ball below as the whole problem, we can see how we can cover as much of this problem. In this case, we know the player is struggling to run with any pace and at times is left behind in games.

Now we will see where we are. If we only add the coach's knowledge from the football aspect and take a minute to think about what you now see, this could be about any problem you have to solve.

You can see that we have two coaches who think along the same way which is great, but can we stretch

the knowledge needed with the two to find the correct solution for the running concerns they have for the player. We can still see from the grey ball example that the problem has been covered in a small area and that a lot of the grey (problem) is not been looked at. Now as coaches, this is where writing the problem statement down and putting it up on the wall will help to visualise what is needed. It will also get other types of people from not only demographic diversity but cognitive diversity as they will look at it from their thoughts, insights, and prospectives.

Also you can start writing around the problem on the wall to review at a later date and understand what you need to do in order to solve the problem, who is needed to solve the problem, and how we are going to solve the problem (action plan). We will learn about the SMARTA objectives in a later chapter. Yes,

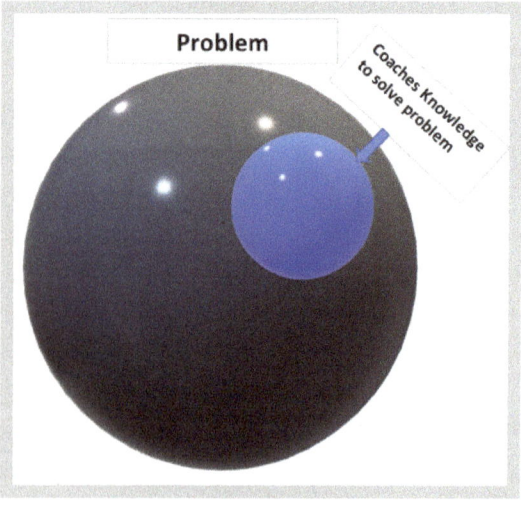

SMARTA as I have designed the SMART objective we all know and love with an added A.

We agree that more help is needed to cover and get correct actions done to help improve the player. So we invite the physio to take a look at the player and ask them for input through their expertise in the world of physiotherapy. They now add to our wall some good ideas around the body and muscles movement and give us some food for thought. Below is the problem in grey with the coaches and physio involved in finding the solution to improve the players running performance.

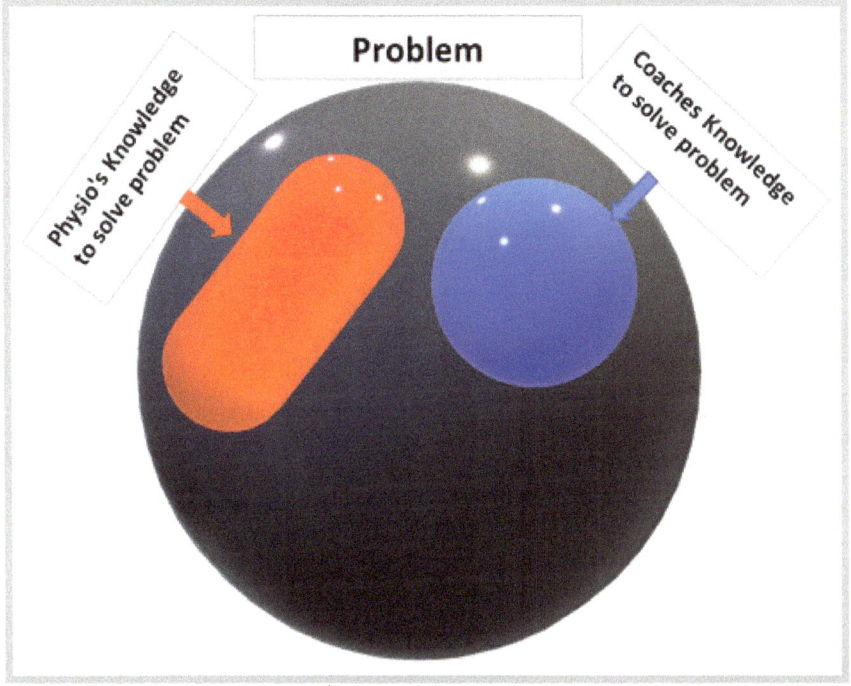

You can now see that we are covering more of the problem but still have a large of the grey area. We now need to look at how to fill this space so that we set up the most diverse team to understand the problem and solve how we are going to deliver it through the action plan.

We decide that the running action is not helping the player and decide to bring in a running coach to get their thoughts and insights to help solve the problem.

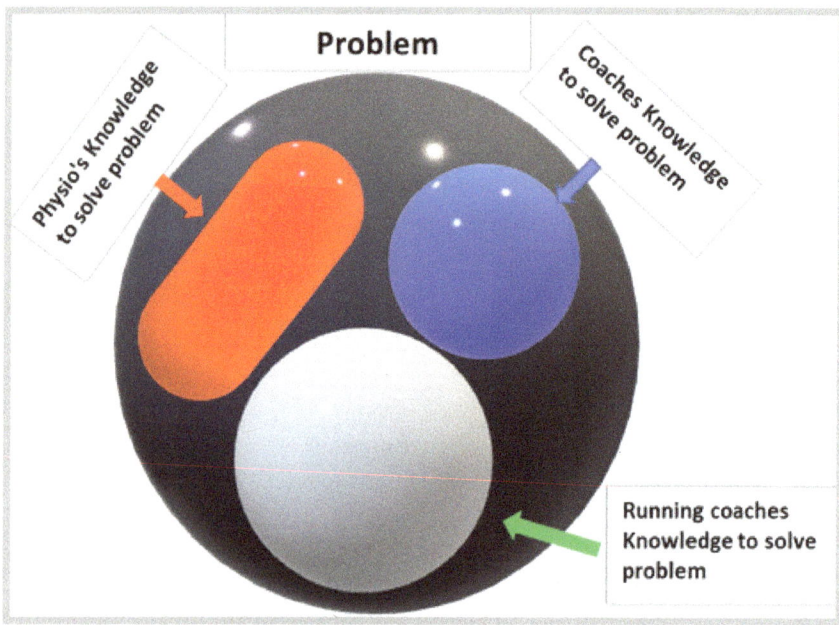

Now we can see that almost all the grey has been covered with different sporting backgrounds and most important, different thoughts and insights to the problem.

You will find that if you start with the problem statement, you will understand what you think and feel is needed to tackle it with all the corners covered, and make better and more rewarding action plans for your players.

REMEMBER

Demographic diversity: The first and most commonly used of the two types is the demographic diversity. This is where we have a difference in race, gender, and class.

Cognitive diversity: The second part of diversity is the cognitive diversity. This is where we have a difference in thoughts, insights, and perspectives.

Chapter 9: The 5 Ws and 1 H

This is a tool I have used for years in business and applied to my coaching journey. It has helped me solve so many problems. It is a part of Kaizen which means small steps of improvement and is from the Toyota production system or TPS for short.

The following diagram shows what are the 5 Ws and 1 H:

The first W is **Who**. When we look at it in coaching terms, we can ask the questions say, if we have a problem with a coach in a team and his qualifications.

Who does it: level two qualified coach

Who is doing it: a level 1 coach

Who should be doing it: a level two coach

Who else can do it: level two and above

Who else should do it: any coach above level 1

The second W is **What** and if using the same example as above.

What to do: Coach to the required level

What is being done: Coaching not to level required.

What should be done: Follow level two coach practice.

What else can be done: bring in correct level of coach.

What else should be done: Bring coach to correct level with training plan.

The third W is **Where** and using the problem above. Not all the W or H are a problem as you will see with Where.

Where to do it: On a surface safe and big enough for session.

Where is it done: At clubs ground.

Where should it be done: At clubs ground.

Where else can it be done: Any surface safe and big enough.

Where else should it be done: Nowhere else.

The fourth W is **When** and we will apply it to the same problem on qualification.

When to do it: Straight away

When is it done: to be arranged

When should it be done: to be at required level for what team needs

What other time can it be done: Straight away.

What other time can it be done: no other time if he wants to stay as coach.

The fifth and final W is **Why** and we will use it with the same problem as above.

Why does he can do it: Coach might know the level but needs qualification for insurance

Why do it: Required law

Why do it there: Only place to do it

Why do it then: Need to get qualification as soon as possible

Why do it that away: Coaching standard from FA

The one and only H is the How and again we will use it with the same problem.

How to do it: Online and in person

How is it done: over a 6-day course

How should it be done: Before you start coaching team

Can this method be used in other areas: Yes

Is there any other way to do it: No

After going through all the questions with the problem statement, we see that the main area to look at is the WHO and WHY, and the HOW to guide us through the sustainment and the potential route causes as in this case, why has the coach not taken the correct level and how has it got missed the club. But more important is we need to get a good coach through this method as a team/club and get the team back on track.

Think about your children or if players are young, why do they keep asking the "why" question. The answer is because they are curious to learn and understand. As we get older and have a lot more knowledge, we find less time to ask the why question. Make it a point to ask the why question because as that great philosopher said "they are only easy if you know the answer" (Chris Tarrant who wants to be a millionaire). BRING THAT INNER CHILD BACK.

Chapter 10: Smarta Objectives

You may have hear of the term SMART which stands for Specific, Measurable, Achievable, Realistic, and Time bound. Well, let me tell you this is good, but not great and I feel missing one final letter – the letter A for "added value".

I will explain why it is the most important letter in the word SMARTA and not SMART.

Let's take an example for both SMART and SMARTA.

A coach of a football team decides to teach his team how to play the piano for improving the team performance.

I see you thinking, "Why good get that inner child out?" and you are right to think this way. Now let's look at it from the SMART objective, to see if it works:

Specific: Teach the players how to play piano, so to become a better team.

Measurable: We can use tests and teachers report.

Achievable: Agree at the time needed from players and teacher to get to the level.

Realistic: Can the players learn the piano? Make sure they learn at their own speed.

Time: Teacher sets the time scale for learning the piano.

Now, I hear your brain going over. But how does this make them play better or become a better team. The coach used the SMART objectives but as I said at the start of the chapter, the important letter missing is the letter A for Added value.

Added value is what we get from the activity that will help, in this case, making the team play better or make them a better team. If you go through this you would see that the added value part brings up questions like "how does the piano playing make a better team?" and "could this time be spent on an area to help the players and the team?"

So, let's look at this again from the side of added value and the word SMARTA.

Statement "How can the team improve?"

Specific: We are going to get professional advice on areas that the team can get some short, medium, and long-term wins.

Measurable: Set up a folder with a sign off for each step and feedback from the professional coaches.

Achievable: Set standard for short, medium, and long-term improvements after understanding where the team is against expectations.

Realistic: This is set with the first three letters and need adjusting as we go.

Time: Professionals to help set time needed with fat built in for areas that take a bit longer to learn.

Added Value: So, now we see that this gives the players the short, medium, and long-term benefits to help improve their games and make the team stronger as a unit.

So, when looking at doing something to improve or benefiting your players or team, think of added value as this will allow the other letters to do a more efficient job.

Chapter 11: Sharing Factual Knowledge

This chapter is all about the factual side of knowledge and not the opinion side.

It is true to say I have lost many hours in listening to people who have no factual knowledge about the game and situation they talk about. But like all coaches, I just seem to come back for more.

The number of times parents and players make statements with no facts behind them and don't get me wrong. We all have an opinion, but only the facts really matter when making big decisions around the way we coach.

I always say to people in the right way, "Your opinion and my opinion doesn't matter, what are the facts telling us" and this allows you as a coach to make better decisions in a timelier manner.

Also, don't be scared to share these facts with others as the days off not sharing knowledge and trying to be the king is slowly going and people will promote get behind those who share. If we go back even only 5 to10 years, the attitude in business and sports was to not share knowledge as this makes me look the fountain of knowledge. Whereas today especially in the football world, more facts are available from different types of experts and these people are willingly sharing their findings with the public through social media.

With this fact-sharing world, we can see today on the Internet there are other reasons for sharing and the main one is greed. They would have you put money and they want you to sign up or pay for everything and don't get me wrong if the service is real and benefits you as a coach or person then we can see the added value. Check out the people you buy from and make sure you get references from others before you commit to spending your hard-earned money. Trust me, not everyone is after a quick buck plenty of people who give up their time for free, who have a lot of good facts about coaching and life.

Facts, well this is a great subject as with most facts they are not facts, but we believe they are. "Hey, what does this mean? Make sense Jason, please!" I hear you saying. Well, let's take a football situation where the team let's in four goals and all the parents and players say the defence has not played well. So this fact is based on what? Yes, you got opinion of one or two parents with the word spread by the others as how can he be wrong? He knows everything. But these facts are not actually facts, they are opinions. Now after the game, the coach gets his report on the game and the true facts, so on all four goal we lost the ball at in the opponents goal box. I have a saying to my players – when we attack we need it to have three outcomes:

1. **Goal**
2. **Corner**
3. **Goal Kick**

What do I mean by this? My teams play through the thirds, attack from the back, and defend from the front. So we commit a lot of numbers forward and this can leave us two on two at the back.

1. **Goal** allows us as a team to celebrate and walk back to the half way.
2. **Corner** allows the team to stay high and look to attack again.
3. **Goal kick** allows the team to stay high and set up ready to win the ball high and start the attack again.

The issue with losing the ball in the last third whilst committing players is straight forward. After a while they get tired and then mistakes happen. so as we say in problem solving, the route cause was ball lost last third and non-detection is back two not coping with numbers on them.

False facts or not facts at all, but we as humans like to follow. So as a coach, take on the true facts and squash any talk that doesn't have factual data behind it. It is ok to have an opinion but that's all, it is just an opinion.

You may think your players would know about the goal, corner, and goal kick. But I tell you, "no, they won't" and for most match days, remind them of this making it easier for yourself and your teammates by looking after that ball and the one outcome for your attacking players is not to give the ball away cheap.

Just remember the facts, where they come from. Can you see evidence on these facts or proof?

Just putting the facts in the Internet's Google Search brings over 68 million links and that is a fact not opinion. Lol!

So as coaches to record information for review at a later date, is a great idea and if you can get data-driven people into your coaching staff this would make a great difference to you when making decisions.

Coaches take a minute to think about the different ways to share these facts. In today's society, we have many options, e-mails are a common way where we send players' or parents' information to be stored and kept for later dates. Also for instant information, WhatsApp groups are very popular. Sending match and training day details and availability is a great way to share facts and information. The good old phone still works wonders and you can all hear the emotions from the other person. Still my favourite way is face to face meetings as this is personal and you get words, tone, and body, and can see and hear all.

So to put it into facts, you need to do a lot of research at times to make sure whatever you are saying as a coach is factual and not misleading. It takes hours for coaching and understanding the data from this coaching, as when you go on a training to improve your coaching, these hours will off been done for you so the information presented is factual and rewarding for developing your next steps in your coaching journey.

Chapter 12: The 3 Ws and WIN

What went well

What went wrong

What improvements needed.

Now before we get in to this part, most people think that "What went well" is a positive point and the "what went wrong" is a negative point. But the facts are they are both positive if used the right way, they will give you areas to improve straight away and for long term.

We can use this technique for training and games. I want to start with using it during the game. The time to ask these two questions is during half time and full time of the game, and we will start at half time as we get to see if what we found out had a solution and if applied how it impacted the results.

We have all sat in the changing room during the half time and heard the coach say when losing 3-0 that was rubbish and they start pointing out all the concerns they have and some even shout at the people they blame.

"You did this, and you did that wrong and it's not good enough blah blah blah…" as it ends up falling on deaf ears. When you want to use the command technique to coach, it has very little effect on players as that's all they ever hear.

So, let's look at this as a scenario. It is half time and we are down 3-1. This is how I would look at handling it. Firstly, I would allow players to have a few minutes to calm down and let them talk about the first half. When I feel the chat is dying out step in, ask them to focus on what I'm about to say. For me, I start with "what went well". So, we get them feeling the good emotions they have had in the game. These would be key moments in the game – good tackle, pass, shoots, but the key one is let's re-live the goal and get them to tell me their thoughts and then give mine. "Lads, we got the goal because we played through the thirds and got the ball out wide. Then looked at playing the ball into feet where our 9 made the perfect 6 yard run and tapped the ball in and all half when we have got the ball out wide 6 or 7 times very look like scoring. So keep this going, but can we do it more please?"

So it is very positive and got them focused on "what went well" and you will find it easier now to talk about the "what went wrong" side.

So, let's talk about "what went wrong" and make sure you do this in a calm manner as the players will pick up if you show stress, anger, or any other emotion. I prefer to sit with your players at times and ask simple questions as saying rubbish only frustrates them more and they know it was poor but need the magic answers and solutions to solve these problems.

Just diverting a little, it reminds me of a coach I watched at a local men's game screaming at his players "DO SOME THING". Lol! Do something? Well, they are! Even if it is wrong. It made me laugh for a week and still does while typing these words. But on a serious note he would be much better giving these players an instruction that will help them solve the problem.

Going back to "what went wrong", I would look at the three goals and not always the last part of the goal or as I call it the non-detection side. But the "where it started" is the root cause and a talk through how we can stop this happening with the team and individuals is required. Let's say this is what happened in my eyes.

"Lads take the first goal. They had a corner and we didn't put the first blocker in place on the six-yard box and they had a near post runner who headed it on the run. Whose man was this? I know it but I want ownership. If you allow players to make mistakes without being shouted at or made to feel small, they will put their hands up. But remember what I said. This is the non-detection side and the route cause from the corner is we didn't set up as we should. My next question is who is in charge of the set up for defensive corners. This is where my keeper puts his hands up as he knows through many hours of trainings, he scans and makes sure all players start in the correct position. This is very important as the old saying goes "shit in shit out".

The second and third goals were both penalties and given away from the same player, our number 3. This is where I ask him what he should be looking to do against a very quick winger and he replies, "delay denies dictate" As we know forwards love to not have to think when going for a goal and just act on instinct. The last question I have for him is where did the situation take place and he replies, "15 meters outside the box." So again, getting him to think if the same challenge happened outside the box the result would be a free kick and not a penalty (twice). So hopefully, this player understands that the root cause for penalty was not making decision to tackle before the winger entered the box. If he delayed the player help could have been arriving in time to double up on the winger. Also from a coaching side, could I have given the message to him before the half time chat, maybe we would have only conceded one goal and be 2-1 down at half time.

Of course, we came back and won 10-3, lol!

Now the ""what went well" and "what went wrong" at full time are both very different but actually are the same questions, as we can no longer change the result but maybe prepare for the next training session or players ring for a chat.

Take the same game and look at how we controlled the game and scored so many goals. First I let the players settle down from being very excited after the win and get them focused on the "what went wrong". The reason I start this way round is that the lads are on a high and need to be kept high but not too high.

Not a lot of time should be spent on this but lads bring up first half and I step in and say actual that's what went well part as you will see in a minute. So we move on to "what went well" and the first part the players talked about was "how well we got the ball out to both wings" This lead to 6 off the goals we scored and how the other four came from set piece that we set up right and delivered. Our number 3 said he got the fast winger to stop as he delayed him again and again until the winger got so frustrated he lost his game and was subbed and the new winger had nowhere near the pace of the first winger.

I make the point of saying all I did was give you the problem statement through facts and together we put together the WIN "what improvements needed" plan and I will talk about that next.

I also make sure I thank the boys not for the win but the way they solved the problems at their own level as if players understand the why they can find the how.

Now take the same two questions into training and they might be about the session that was planned from the areas of improvement needed from the game. The time to ask these questions is just after the finish after they have cooled down and having a drink and again don't ask close ended questions where the players will answer yes no you need open ended questions, few examples below of closed ended and open-ended questions. I have left a gap between questions, so you can write your answers below.

- Are you feeling better today?
- May I use the bathroom?
- Is the prime rib a special tonight?
- Should I date him?
- Will you please do me a favour?
- Have you already completed your homework?
- Is that your final answer?
- Were you planning on becoming a fireman?
- Should I call her and sort things out?
- Is it wrong to want to live on my own at this age?
- Shall we make dinner together tonight?
- Could I possibly be a messier house guest?
- Might I be of service to you ladies this evening?
- Did that man walk by the house before?
- Can I help you with that?
- May I please have a bite of that pie?
- Would you like to go to the movies tonight?
- Is math your favourite subject?
- Does four plus four equal eight?
- Is that haunted house really scary?
- Will you be going to Grandmother's house for Christmas?
- Did Dad make the cake today?

- Is there a Mass being held at noon?
- Are you pregnant?
- Is he dead?

Now, look at the answers you have written, and you will see they are just Yes or No, and this is what closes the question.

Now, let's look at what open ended questions look like answer each question, so you can review and reflect on the amount of information you get.

- What were the most important wars fought in the history of the United States?
- What are you planning to buy today at the supermarket?
- How exactly did the fight between the two of you start?
- What is your favourite memory from childhood?
- How will you help the company if you are hired to work for us?
- What do you plan to do immediately following graduation from college?
- What types of decorations do you plan to have for your friend's birthday party?
- What was your high school experience like?
- How did you and your best friend meet?
- What sights do you expect to see on your vacation?
- How do you go about booking tickets for a flight?
- What were the major effects of World War II for the United States?
- How do you go about purchasing a home?
- What is it like to live in Morocco?
- What is the quickest way to get to the pet store in town?
- Why is it that every time I talk with you, you seem irritated?
- How could I present myself better?
- How do you manage to raise your children alone?
- What is the matter with the people in that class?
- Where are you going to find the time to write all those letters?
- Why can't I come along with you?
- What makes the leaves change colour?
- How exactly does one replace the screen to a cellular phone?

See how these open-ended questions start with a what, why, where, and how. We have already used these in an earlier chapter.

Read your answers and it will be plain to see you will have much more detailed and better answers.

So, when putting into football questions, here's a couple, one closed and one open:

Did the winger go around you? Yes, and we knew what was benefit if anything the player has been called out.

Why did the winger go around you? Because I did not react quick enough to the situation and should have pressed the player and made him delay, so support could arrive instead. But I backed off until I was in the box and mistimed my tackle.

I know which one I would like to hear back from the player, remember the why, what, where, and how when starting your question and this will engage your players.

The session might have been just to go over set piece shape or a new technique or skill. But great to ask the lads, "what went wrong" and "what went well".

WIN (WHAT IMPROVEMENT NEEDED)

So, all we talked for "what went wrong" and "what went well" falls into the "WIN" – what improvement needed. We all know people whether they bare parents, players, or fans who have a problem for every solution (lol!) and not a solution for every problem and by using the WIN analogy.

Think about it in the last chapter, we get the WIN answers by following the "what went wrong" and "what went well".

If you set out following these simple questions and structure your half time, full time, and end of training in this format, the players will understand and buy in.

Chapter 13: The 12th Man – A WADES

A WADES is my 12th man and a way to get the team to remember these Non-negotiables.

So, who is this 12th man we have in the team? You might never see his name on the team sheet, but he is woven into the fabric of the team and helps to drive the culture and requirements needed to improve the players.

We will talk about A WADES in more detail but first let's start by letting you all know what it stands for:

As One

Work rate

Attitude

Desire

Enjoyment

Shape

These for me as a coach and person are non-negotiable and they help built my philosophy that I deliver with my players, parents, club members, and fans. We are going to work through these letters and learn what I mean by this 12th man.

As one:

Now, most of the people will say the same old same old we do as I say as coach and all buy into it but there lies the problem. This is one person's vision and not a team effort/club effort. I call this a dictatorship and we know where it has got many people. So I see this as a very strong lesson I learned as a young Plant Manager in a big, busy automotive business. Whilst working with the union, I watched them try and agree on a pay rise. If you have ever been involved with or are a part of a union, you will know how this works. The people in the union come together and agree as a collective on what they want to present to the company, and the representatives of the union will take the business leaders for a meeting and try to agree on an amount that both parties are happy with.

What I noticed was a very strong person leading the union and the word on the street was the people wanted 2.5% pay rise but he wanted 5%. When they came to the meeting he put the 5% forward, which was not the collective's agreement but his own opinion and it was rejected. The talks went for over a month for over a month with neither side budging until I decided to call the union in and ask them how they got to the 5% figure.. Once it was known about the percentage and what the majority wanted, I used true facts to let them know that the national average for the year was 1.5%, so the 2.5% was over the average and that would be what we offered to all members as the majority wanted this in the first place. As you can imagine, this went through straight away. I suppose my point and the lesson learned was that if you are a team, you work as a team. Yes you have a philosophy, but part of that is team work, sharing, giving and taking. Don't just listen but understand others.

Once you all agree on the way forward or actions, then lock in the **as one**.

Work Rate

For me as a coach, this is another area that has a huge impact on the culture and quality of the players, and the direction they will go, as we see players running much further than 5 years ago and even more if you go back 10 years. Don't get me wrong, we have lost a lot of the art, by the way, the game has developed and with the search for success and the amount of money to find this success, the game will only get quicker.

We will talk about work rate on the pitch as this is what most people think about when they hear it but what does this mean off the pitch.

The rate at which work is done.

"The work rate of the checkout assistants"

The amount of energy that is expended in sport or physical exercise.

"His work rate and tackling were to his normal standards"

So, we can look at work rate of the coaching staff, and the players can see this. So if they see the coaching staff working hard, completing tasks and deadlines, they will want to have the same on field and off field attitude and work rate. So if we look at it not as "how quick" but "how far" then we will see the different types of work rates that are needed, as it would be no good for a 100-meter athlete who has been trained hard and had a high work rate to be told, "today you are running a marathon" They would look great for 100 meters, lol, then struggle. So when we look at work rate use the SMARTA objective and remember to check if it gives added value.

On field, my players know we look at high intensity and that we are out of possession as individual's way more than in possession. So what we do without the ball is very important and when in possession, we need to make sure that we use the possession wisely with the work rate and try to make correct decisions.

Attitude

As coaches, we know this can be the most draining area to coach but it also can be the most rewarding. Most of the people look at others and judge them on attitude, but a couple of major points here are to look at your attitude and understand your players before judging their attitude. So, what does this mean?

We never sit down and think about our own attitude very often or if at all, that takes time to reflect on key moments of your day maybe work or football, as if you understand yourself (self-awareness) better then you will be able to handle issues better. Don't be scared to ask people how they see you and your attitude. Don't just ask this to people you like or who like you, but ask the ones who are a bit stand offish with you because they might have some great learning points to help you develop. In business, we call it 360 degrees but set a few questions, not of closed type, and make them feel that they can be open with answers. You can even do a little survey where they don't have to leave a name but can share what they see and feel.

Now, once you have the understanding of where you are to people and what you feel makes a good attitude, you can start to explain this to your players and parents, and see if they agree (as one). And once the information is locked in to brain by players and parents, you can start to access them and find ways to help them see these areas to improve and together develop ways to work on these. Don't try to change everything straight away (remember the 4 Ts of change) as this can take time and hard work.

Remember, it is easy to say good or poor attitude, but you will need to define what a good and poor attitude looks like as an individual and group.

Desire

This is my favourite topic and it is needed to be watched carefully as my passion can sometimes get in the way of what is desire for others. I have a true story and this helps to shape my views on desire.

You find this example at work. When people get a promotion, it is likely the loud ones who rise to the top and sometimes don't fit the role but still get the role. I was once looking to put in place a new supervisor for an area of the factory and had 5 or 6 people come to me saying they were applying for it and they mentioned why they should get the role. I had one person who got someone else to ask me if they could have a chat with me. At that time I thought, "Well, if they can't come over their self then by what chance can they think of running a team in the factory? How closed minded of me!

I did arrange a chat with them and found them to be a very good communicator. They understood what was required from the role and were very strong on the business side. They also understood the KPIs and what it meant to deliver quality and cost, to our customers. They knew themselves that they needed a bit of training in leadership but that was my job to sort it out, so I told them to apply and I will interview them.

As you can imagine they got the role and did very well at it and have developed into a great senior manager.

The moral of this story is doesn't be scared to look under the rocks for desire as not all desire comes in the form of loud and energetic. Talk to the players that are quite as you will find they have a true love for the game and make sure you get the group to understand that being quite does not mean you don't have desire in what you are trying to achieve. Remember the 4 types of people? Exactly.

Don't mistake winning with desire as you see it more when teams are losing, and players struggle but understand the type of person and what desire looks like to them.

Enjoyment

What a word and if we are honest this is why we play this beautiful game but understand what enjoyment is to yourself and others as yet again we may have different opinions on the why we enjoy something. |example could be some players love to be around friends and others like to keep fit so get your players and do the exercise of understanding what brings each player enjoyment and don't except winning as that is the output of the input, in this case the enjoyment.

We all do better at anything we try when we enjoy it and one area as a coach to develop yourself and the players is to be opened minded to trying new ideas or change and apply as a coach the 4 T's of change because being **transparen**t with your players on what you plan to do allows you to give them the **truth** on what you are going to do and expect the **time** needed to complete the task and they will **trust** you even more.

I say coaches must push and encourage players to smile more and laugh as it is still one of the best sights you will see anywhere.

Shape

It can sometimes be thought of as your philosophy, but you can play many formations and shapes to a philosophy. This subject is widely covered, and you can out of possession play a high press, medium block, low block but once playing one off these it is your job as a coach to get them to understand the shape of these blocks and what you are trying to achieve. For me the achievement is firstly to slow the opponents down. Let's take the high press this only works if the players all go together and we want to steal the ball high up the pitch and play from there, with the medium block we need to design a shape that doesn't allow the ball to be played through the lines, and the low block again not allowing the opponents to exploit in behind the players and force them to shoot from distance or win the ball and attack.

Players watch the game on TV and as do parents but to truly understand the effort and commitment these players on TV put in to understand what is needed to break down the oppositions game and get the shape in attack that is needed to win games is huge.

People think you win the ball and run down the pitch and score I wish lol and at times it may even look this way to the human eye, but all the players understand their roles and know the shape.

Hour after hour goes in on patterns of play and if you watch the top level you can see players don't need to look as they know where their team mates will be as they must hold their shape. A big part of coaching is to be repetitive, but we can blend this in different ways during training through rondo's or small sided games or even the drills we put together.

When watching games on the TV a good exercise is to see if you can work out the formations they are playing and what formation they take in a defensive role and then attacking role and the shape will allow them to go from defense to attack or vice versa and see how quickly the transition takes.

We can see how important the 12th man A WADES is to the team and our coaching and how much work is needed to truly understand the letters in his name and what they mean to you as a coach and to your players and parents as for me to understand something allows you to accept issues and find ways to fix and even improve.

Not everything we do needs to cost a fortune and below are some simple vales that are free, and everyone possess them if they want. They also require no talent so just by putting these 10 words into practice will help make you a better person and player or coach.

1. Be on time
2. Work ethic
3. Effort
4. Body Language
5. Energy
6. Attitude
7. Be coachable
8. Passion
9. Doing extra
10. Be prepared.

Most of these words have come out in the chapters you have already read but as simple as they are they are very easy to forget and full back into bad habits so let's look at the technique that looks at the good and that bad on each of these words and this will give you an idea of when done right not a lot goes on as expected but if done wrong then the impact can be massive.

Number one **"be on time"** now this is a pet hate of mine as I've never been on time let alone late my view is set out with plenty of time in hand and plan your day to allow you to be on time and when all the players are on time the day starts in the correct manner and you can leave or start on time but when we are not on time then think about this scenario and how it makes you feel and the people around you.

Team are asked by the coach to meet at the club for 10am so they can get on the road for 10.15 and they know the ground they are travelling to is 30 minutes away and want a good 60 minutes to warm up for the game that kicks off at 12 o'clock and yes this still gives us 15 extra minutes as we don't control the traffic. We have 15 lads in the team and at 10am 13 are at the club and we are waiting for 2 so at 10.5 I contact the parents to ask where they are, and they tell me running a little bit late they eventually get to the club for 10.20 and what makes it worse they seem to find it funny.

Now as much as I want to talk to them I feel it more important to get going and deal with it after the game. We arrive at the game at 11.05 so 5 minutes behind where we need to be but good job we put a bit of fat in the timings and don't have to rush anything.

After the game when all sat in the bar I had a chat with the players and asked what their views are about being late and they both replied nothing we can do as we don't drive, and I get this but nothing? Not sure and I asked them can you not sit with your parents and tell them how important it is to you to be on time as it's part of the prep and also you don't want to let your team mates down, also what about sending a text to the coach as at least he knows you are ok and on your way.

Now the hard art talking with the parent and again think about the re-framing technique we talked about and you don't want to close them off or make them angry so think about talking about the game and how you thought their child played to open them up and them let them know how important to their child and you it is to be on time when possible and the life lessons this teaches them for work and play.

We have covered work rate, but **work ethics** are different as this is about what we believe in as a team and how we deliver these ethics every time and again when done to the agreed standards works like clock work but if people don't this can again cause divide within the team take our view on leaving the changing room the way we found it and we have a Rota that gives players and coaches a direct direction and plan on who's turn it is and how we expect this to be done and one of the players decides he doesn't feel like it as it is not his job.

This would be for me an area we need to correct straight away as one we don't want other people thinking this is ok or the standard we set and I would sit the player down and ask him why he has not done it and go through those reasons and also go through the reasons we set this standard and the one voice policy we all agreed to at the beginning of the season.

If this doesn't help you then have a decision to make for the team and bigger picture but delivered in the right manner, then there is no reason it will not work.

Effort, now don't get mixed up with ability or talent effort is about giving 100% of what you have and I tell you as a coach this can be very difficult to show people what this means and in the team I coach we have a few players who give 100% every game even if the is a 6 or 7 in performance ratings but I have a few that can range from a 3-9 and this is very hard to work with as a coach as the spread on performance is so wide.

Give me the 6 or 7 any day as we can set up and understand our strengths and weaknesses but when we have the 3 to 9 range it can kill the dynamics of the team.

A big part of effort is how well we listen so if we understand the instruction or task we can deliver it better often. From a coach's point of view it's ok to let them know they are stronger at certain areas than others and even get the strong players helping the weaker players in areas and vice versa when the weaker player now becomes the stronger player on another area of the game letting them self-manage and coach each other is a wonderful sight and great for communication and the players development.

Remember the **body language** chapter about the words and tone and lastly the body language is so important as when we are winning you can tell from the coaches body language as you can when we are losing but remember that the players need more help when losing as they want that reassurance that all is ok and not a coach with his head in his hands shouting nothings to his player think about your impact on the players and parents so can you stand up smile and give meaningful information to players so they can solve issues and get back into the game.

It can be very hard to be energetic all the time so make sure you know when you can relax and when you need to show the **energy** needed to motivate your players and staff.

Another area where energy comes in different packages and knowing your players gives you a better understanding of what energy means to them.

Attitude now lots of time we have touched on this in this book and that's because it means so much to me as a coach and person and if I can show the right attitude then so can my player and this will help to develop them for the future and we all know what a bad attitude can do for a team it needs to be operated on straight away or if you can't fix then remove.

Below is a great quote about ATTITUDE and makes a very true point in my philosophy towards the game.

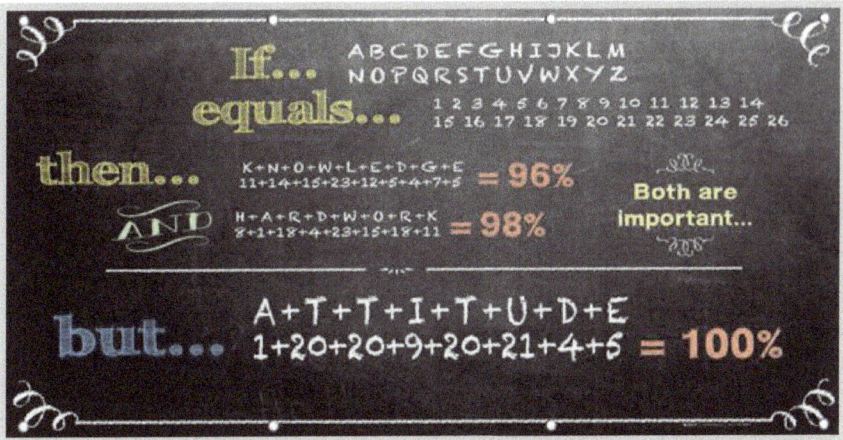

Being Coachable. Now what does this mean? Let's start with the coaching side. Can we learn new ways and apply these learnings, watch other coaches, and pick up the good or bad? You see it's all learning by following other sports and coaches, and even from the players we have now. We have all meet those coaches who know everything about everything and are closed minded to being coached by others. But what they don't understand is that they did learn at some point and decided to stop learning as their self-awareness changed and ended up being a cost of high. Remember the EQ chapter on the 15 behaviours. Players, well this is no different and we can see the players hungry for more knowledge and the ones who we do the learning, and they might not be your stars today, but they will be tomorrow and, in my eyes, they are already a star as they have what is needed to develop and climb higher.

We all know players that have passion and hear people say, "He plays with such passion". But what does that mean. Well for me, it's easy, firstly, they enjoy what they are doing and secondly, they know what they do and how to do it. If a player shows a lack of passion, it is a trigger for the coach to go and find out why. Especially, if the player has shown loads of passion perversely, you will find they are not happy

You first need to understand what is making them unhappy. Is it an on-field problem or an off-field problem and the why this has made them unhappy. Then you can start to build and solve the concern using all the tools and people around you.

Doing extra – like the old saying, going the extra mile is very important to you as a coach because not all your work is done in front of a crowd. As the word "integrity" truly means doing things to improve when no one's watching. The things have to be value added. Remember SMARTA the extra A in this.

Players who stay behind to work on the areas of development and even for a chat on trying to understand how they can get better and what they can do to use the time effectively. But those players and coaches who can't be bothered with the extra mile, will always work theway they do and in any work or sports environment. We need to do extra to continue to grow and develop.

Well, are you prepared? If not, **be prepared.** As coaches we have so much to do. It's not just turn up and train or play, but hours go behind the scenes to get what some take for granted.

Just think about a session for players and you need to check balls are pumped up correctly, bibs are clean, you have the correct number of cones, and all the other equipment needed, oh and 6 arms to carry them, lol. Have you ever turned up to training and the lads complain that the balls are flat? Well, that's being prepared but also this can be around the administration side, health and safety, parents, and the list goes on.

It is required to check if the players are hydrated , had enough fuel (food), kit clean and in good condition as this will lead to players not playing well and not understanding the why.

As per an old saying,

"Fail to prepare then prepare to Fail".

Chapter 14: Free Gifts

Some free and easy-to-use gifts for coaching.

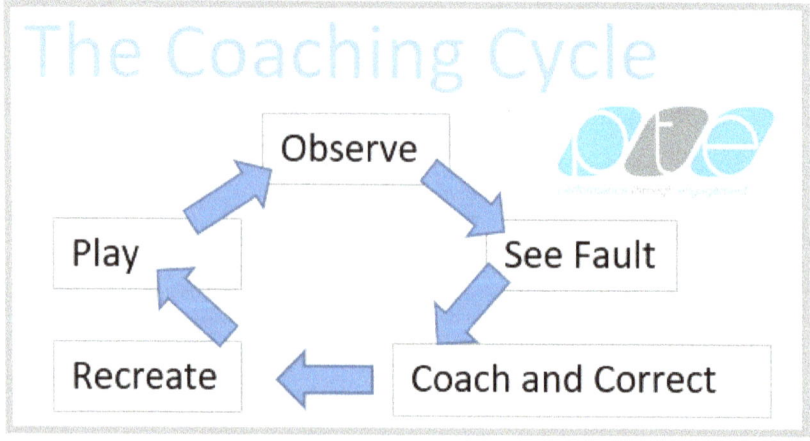

Football EQ For Coaches

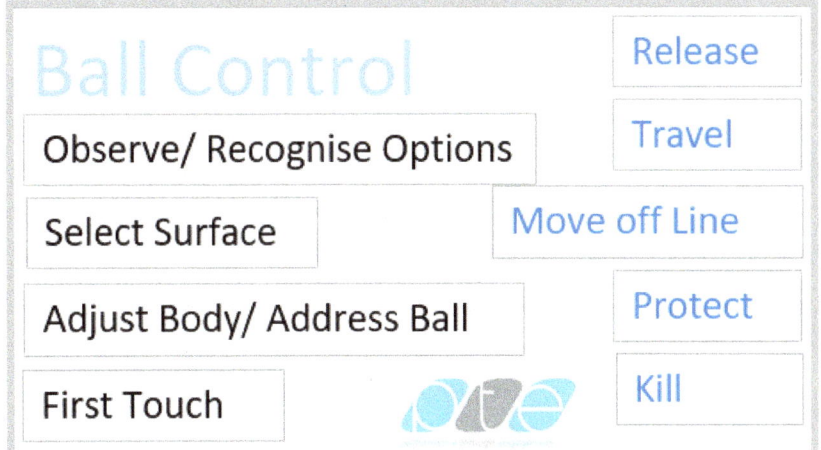

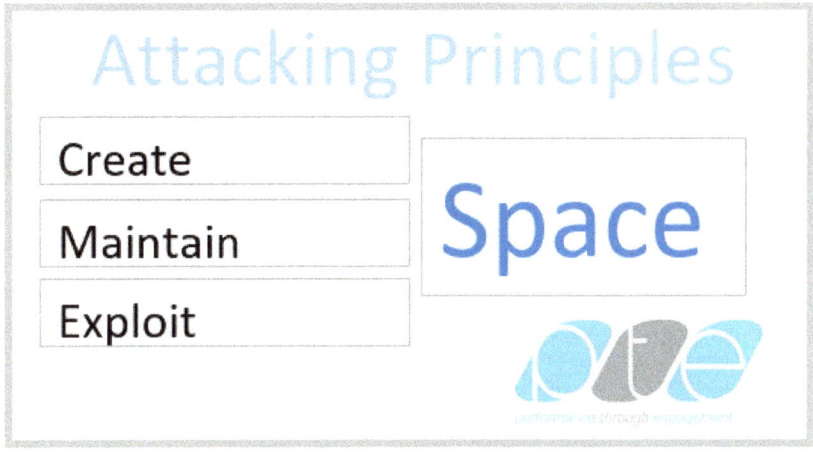

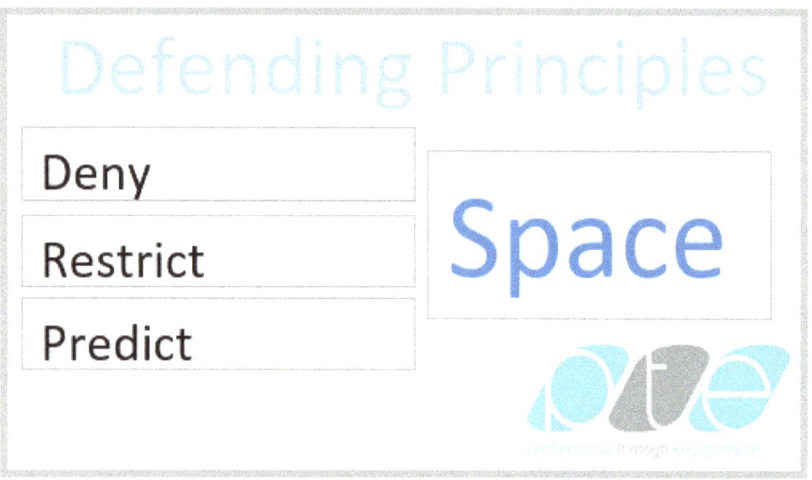

The next gift is the coloured cone memory game. You set 5 different colours in a sized area to suit – Orange, red, blue, yellow, and white and start by giving players an instruction of four colours they have to touch in order. For example red, white, blue, red. You can also give a time restriction if you want to make the game harder.

As the rounds go on and players complete, add a cone to each round. Below are the cards as trying to remembering 5 or 6 plus and coaching is very hard.

4s

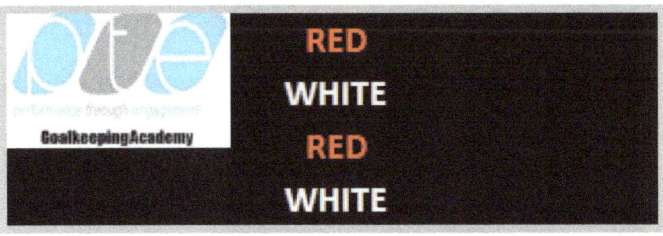

5s

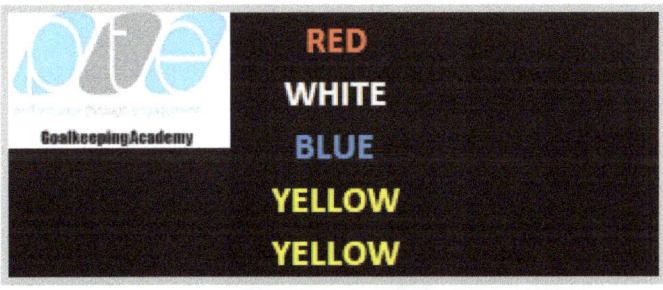

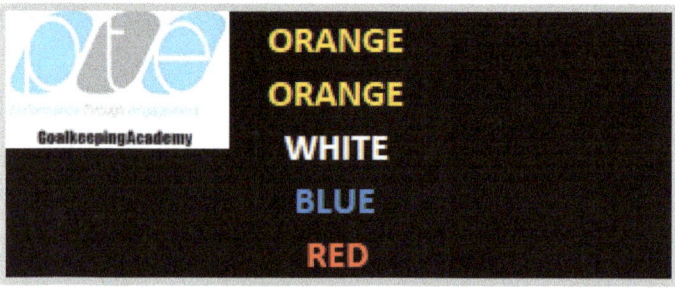

6s

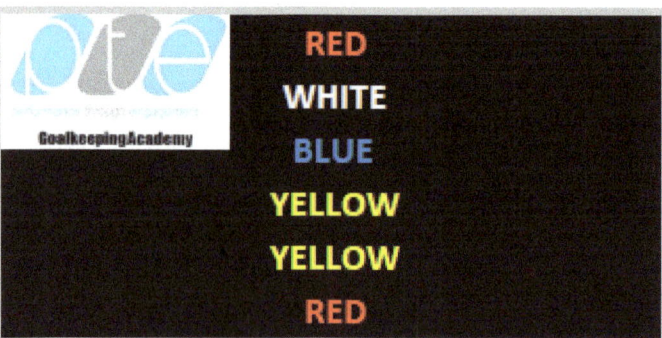

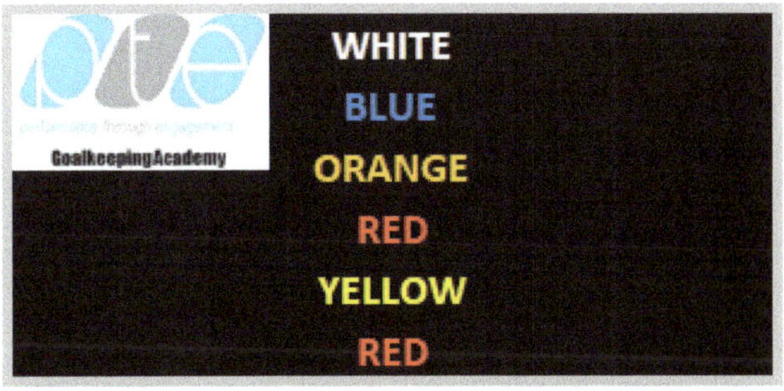

otc Goalkeeping Academy	**WHITE** **BLUE** **ORANGE** **RED** **YELLOW** **RED**
otc Goalkeeping Academy	**ORANGE** **WHITE** **ORANGE** **BLUE** **RED** **WHITE**
otc Goalkeeping Academy	**RED** **WHITE** **YELLOW** **RED** **ORANGE** **BLUE**
otc Goalkeeping Academy	**WHITE** **BLUE** **RED** **ORANGE** **WHITE** **YELLOW**

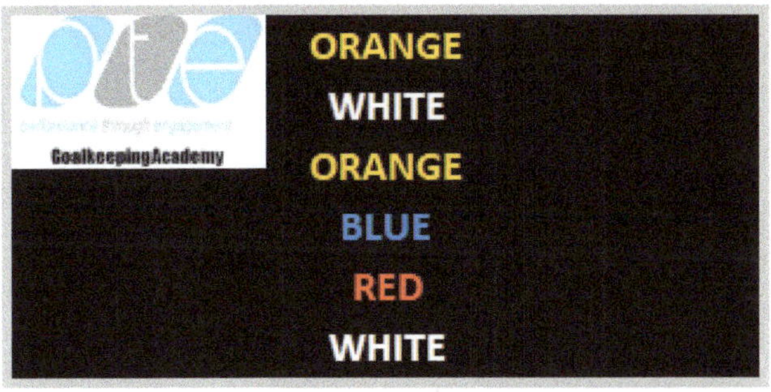

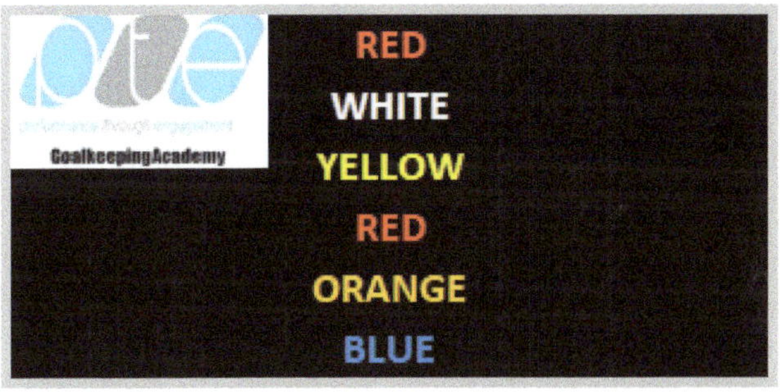

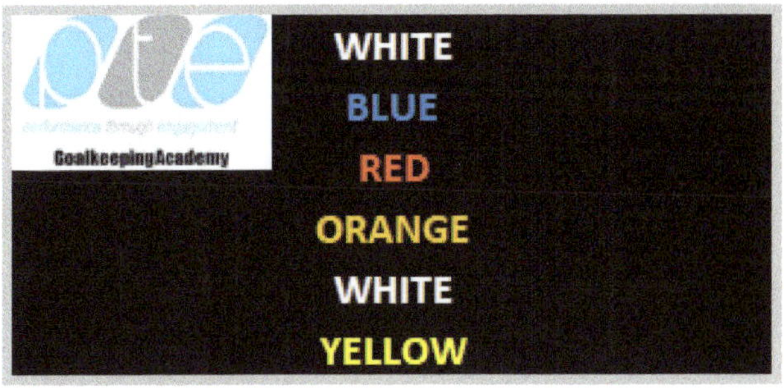

If you want the full excel sheet, just drop me an e-mail quoting "cones excel" at jasonpyott@gmail.com.

Chapter 15: Scouting Player

As a coach, this is a great skill to learn as what does a good player look like to you. You will find some very good courses on the FA website for different levels.

I put together my own type of player questions using the 4 corners when scouting for a new player and you can see the level of questions I ask myself on each and every single scouting mission.

I go through the Technical/tactical side then look at the Psychological side followed by the physical side then lastly the social side so, let's take a look in more detail at each of the corners.

Technical/tactical corner

1. **Attitude to learning:** Can the player learn new skill and how long does it take to learn and then apply in training and games?

2. **High skill level:** Does the player have skills required to move up example in possession and out of possession can he dribble pass or tackle to a high level?

3. **Sound passing:** Can the player understand the different types of passes and when to use then looking for correct weight of pass and when to play forward, side wards, backwards risk over reward?

4. **Touch:** Does the player know when to keep ball tight in those close contact areas and when they can move ball and travel with longer touches so to run freely?
5. **Decision making:** Can the player make decisions for themselves during the training or game to show they understand what is needed?
6. **Control:** Is the first touch good and do they know what part of the body to use when looking to control the ball verbal and nonverbal control as well?
7. **Both feet:** Can the player use both feet when needed in passing, tackling, and shooting/finishing?
8. **Vision:** Does player scan see picture before receiving the ball or receives and then looks at game picture? Can player talk through vision in game and get others to buy in?
9. **Marking:** Can the player decide and make a clear decision when to press and when to back off from marking players do they know the right way to pass on a player and not just point and hope?
10. **Understanding tactics:** Clear to see player is following the tactics and trying to apply the tactics into his game.
11. **Passing:** Does the player know the type of pass required for the area of the pitch the weight and style of pass?
12. **Tactically aware:** Does the player know his surroundings in the game and what strengths and weaknesses the other team has?
13. **Space awareness:** Can the player exploit, maintain, or create space at the right time to give the team an advantage?

Psychological
1. **EQ behaviours:** Does the player keep his emotions under control and use them to help delivery the game's needs?
2. **Mental Strength:** When the game goes wrong can the player find ways within the rules and team culture to be strong and show team mates that they are in control?
3. **Performance under pressure:** Player knows what pressure looks like for position and shows a calm controlled attitude whilst under pressure.

4. **Replicate performance:** Player can play at performance plus or minus 1 as explained in earlier chapter better to be a 7 than a 3-9 builds consistency.
5. **Attitude:** Not important if winning or losing but player shows the right attitude to the team, coach, and opposition as it says **NO DICK HEADS**.
6. **Decision making (In/Out of possession):** Is the player in possession strong enough to hold of players and hold up ball can see the pass required and strength to deliver whilst out of possession the player can work the angles and distance to break or slow down play?
7. **How they approach training:** We have all meet those who train well and play poor and the other way around but when scouting a player, we want the same energy to training as they do in the game.
8. **Willingness to learn:** Do they want to learn from themselves and from others and want to learn is a must?
9. **Willingness to share:** This is a must for me in a player as they all know stuff we don't and the more we share, the stronger the group grows, and this also gives the player plenty of respect from coaches and players.

Physical
1. **Strength:** Can the player hold their own in contact situations and can they show strength in attack and defence?
2. **Quick:** Does player show the right amount of speed and control?
3. **How they train:** Position specific, can they put into practice the physical side they show in games?
4. **Speed:** Position specific for different positions, the player will need to show different types of speed so as a coach understand the position requirements.
5. **Acceleration:** Can the player get off the mark using body strength to drive into full speed?
6. **Agility:** Your player will need to understand and show the agility needed to play in position so can they turn, move off the mark, and change directions.

7. **Cardiovascular fitness:** Can the player keep up with the training or games pace and to what level are they performing at within the group?
8. **Core-body strength:** Does the player use core to help move and take better positions in training or game as it is very important to stay fit by having a very strong core?
9. **Power:** Power comes in different shapes and sizes and need to look at it in running, in possession, out possession, short distance runs, and longer distance runs.
10. **Movement:** Look for that 360 movement can player play with back to goal and facing whilst moving left right forward and backward.

Social

1. **How many clubs have they played at:** This might sound a strange question but if a player has had lots of clubs and many in a season, you need to understand why this is so? Have a good sit down with them and get them to a talk through this, as it will always raise red flags with me but doesn't mean they don't have good reasons.
2. **Reasons for leaving clubs:** This question will give a better understanding of what the player is looking for and if this fits with your philosophy.
3. **Lifestyle:** Get the player to talk about what they do away from football, so you can understand the lifestyle they lead and if they are approaching the game and life in a good manner.
4. **Like/dislike in football:** Try to understand what the player likes and dislikes about the game and gauge face expressions as if you know what they value and this fits in with your philosophy. It will become easier as you both speak the same language on most football subjects and on the dislikes don't just think if you don't agree well that wrong give the player a chance to explain the why they feel this way and maybe you will not necessary agree but at least understand.
5. **Philosophy on football:** Great to hear what players first of all think a philosophy is and then their version of their philosophy and if it fits within your philosophy you know this

player will understand what you are trying to deliver and buy into it.

6. **Team player:** Listen for words like "we" or "our team" as it is good to get over the "I" side. Also you need to ask them about moments the team has done well and not so well and what part they played in both scenarios.

4 CORNERS - TYPE OF PLAYER
○ AUDIT SHEET SCOUT

TECHNICAL/TACTICAL
- ☐ ATTITUDE TO LEARNING
- ☐ HIGH SKILL LEVEL
- ☐ SOUND PASSING
- ☐ TOUCH
- ☐ DECISION MAKING
- ☐ CONTROL
- ☐ BOTH FEET
- ☐ VISION
- ☐ MARKING
- ☐ UNDERSTAND TACTIC
- ☐ PASSING
- ☐ TACTICALLY AWARE
- ☐ SPACE AWARENESS

PSYCHOLOGICAL
- ☐ EQ BEHAVIOURS
- ☐ MENTAL STRENGTH
- ☐ PERFORMING UNDER PRESSURE
- ☐ REPLICATE PERFORMANCES
- ☐ ATTITUDE (NO DICK HEAD POLICY)
- ☐ DECISION MAKING (IN/OUT OF POSSESSION)
- ☐ HOW THEY APPROACH TRAINING
- ☐ WILLINGNESS TO LEARN } OPEN
- ☐ WILLINGNESS TO SHARE } MIND

PHYSICAL
- ☐ STRENGTH
- ☐ QUICK
- ☐ HOW THEY TRAIN
- ☐ SPEED   } POSITION
- ☐ ACCELERATION   } SPECIFIC
- ☐ AGILITY
- ☐ CARDIOVASCULAR FITNESS
- ☐ CORE - BODY STRENGTH
- ☐ POWER
- ☐ MOVEMENT

PRACTICE AS YOU WANT TO PLAY

SOCIAL
- ☐ HOW MANY CLUBS HAVE THEY PLAYED AT
- ☐ REASON FOR LEAVING CLUBS
- ☐ LIFESTYLE
- ☐ LIKES/DISLIKES IN FOOTBALL
- ☐ PHILOSOPHY ON FOOTBALL
- ☐ TEAM PLAYER

practice makes perfect

Chapter 16: My Philosophy

Wow! So we get to the last chapter. For me the whole point and the reason I wrote this book is that all these ideas and learnings on a journey too long to remember have helped me and others to develop not only as football players but also as people and how they can become better coaches.

The meaning of the word philosophy:

__The study of the fundamental nature of knowledge, reality, and existence, especially when considered as an academic discipline.__

A theory or attitude that acts as a guiding principle for behaviour.

When I built this, I was looking at a definition of my values and what I stand for.

Better understand themselves and of course me.

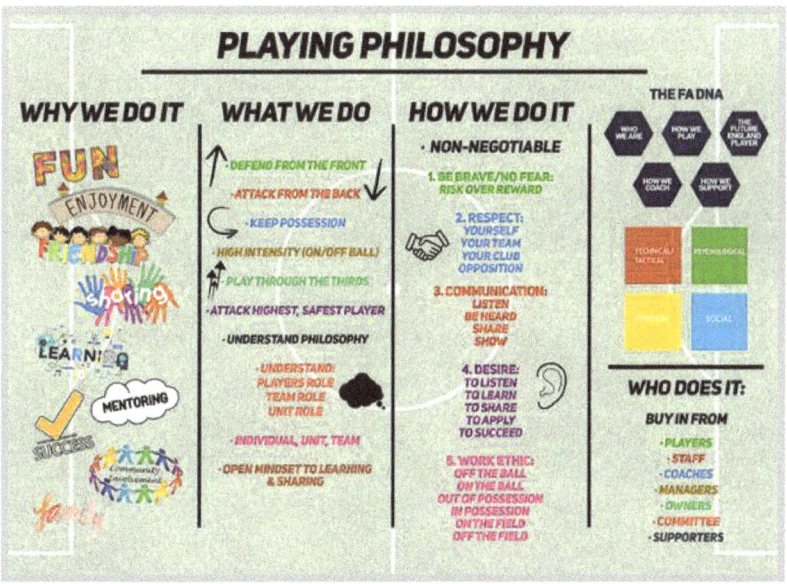

When building what my philosophy is I put together the above visual, so I could do what is important to me and by using the "why we do it", "what we do", "how we do it", and "who does it" gave me a clear vision of my philosophy.

So, the **why we do it** is very clear to me. I want to enjoy it and have fun whilst building new friendships and maintaining these relationships which are already in place, trying to learn as much as we can share any knowledge we have to help others. Strivie to grow that family feeling and bring success to the club and local community and where possible, mentor as many people as we can.

Now for the **what we do** as a team, we will look at a scenario of attacking from the back and defending from the front whilst in possession we want to. When we can play through the thirds keeping the ball and driving high intensity in and out of possession. Knowing how we will play as individuals, units, and a team is very important and will bring an open mindset to learning and sharing, and learn to believe the philosophy.

How we do it – the true values in the way my philosophy works and I call my non-negotiables like being brave, no fear the risk over reward, but always have respect for yourself, team, club, and opposition you will also need to show good communication listen, be heard, share, and show people what you have to offer.

Desire is a major part of my philosophy and what I mean is the desire to, learn, listen, share, apply, and succeed with true work ethics in off the ball, on the ball, out of possession, in possession, on the field, and off course off the field.

The last one in my philosophy is who does it and this is what we build a philosophy for the people we are supporting and trying to deliver the message. When we look at this, it is a wide spectrum of people from a wider range on backgrounds and this will include the players, staff, coaches, managers, owners, committee, and the supporters.

We don't always stop as coaches and take five minutes to see the lives we touch every day. But trust me whatever level you are coaching you are helping people with mental health issues, confidence issues, and you might not even see it but they see you as more than a coach they see you as a mentor, friend, and someone to look up to.

Trust me, it's **"nice to be nice"** and never forget this.
Thank you for taking time to read my book.
Love,
Jason

Ingram Content Group UK Ltd.
Milton Keynes UK
UKHW052140190623
423673UK00010B/83